T0124216

Junior and Elena

Victoria M. Howard

authorHOUSE®

AuthorHouse™
1663 Liberty Drive
Bloomington, IN 47403
www.authorhouse.com
Phone: 1 (800) 839-8640

© 2017 Victoria M. Howard. All rights reserved.

No part of this book may be reproduced, stored in a retrieval system, or transmitted by any means without the written permission of the author.

Published by AuthorHouse 06/21/2017

ISBN: 978-1-5246-9541-5 (sc)
ISBN: 978-1-5246-9539-2 (hc)
ISBN: 978-1-5246-9540-8 (e)

Library of Congress Control Number: 2017908968

Print information available on the last page.

Any people depicted in stock imagery provided by Thinkstock are models, and such images are being used for illustrative purposes only. Certain stock imagery © Thinkstock.

This book is printed on acid-free paper.

Because of the dynamic nature of the Internet, any web addresses or links contained in this book may have changed since publication and may no longer be valid. The views expressed in this work are solely those of the author and do not necessarily reflect the views of the publisher, and the publisher hereby disclaims any responsibility for them.

Other Equine Books Written By

Victoria M. Howard

Meadow Skipper: The Untold Story

Victoria M Howard and Bob Marks

Roosevelt Raceway: Where It All Began

Victoria M. Howard with Billy Haughton and Freddie Hudson

Murray Brown: Book Full and Closed

Victoria M. Howard and Bob Marks

Junior: The Horse That Won the Kentucky Derby

Victoria M. Howard

The Birth of a Racehorse

Victoria M. Howard

*The Adventures of Max and Molly: A Love
Story About a Dog and a Horse*

Victoria M. Howard

Rose Runners: Chronicles of the Kentucky Derby Winners

Victoria M. Howard and Bob Marks

Junior just born . Emma feeding him his milk by bottle

For my mother Vivian

"What he loved in horses is was what he loved in men, the blood and the heat of the blood that ran them. All his reverence and all his fondness and all the leanings of his life were for the ardenthearted and they would always be so and never be otherwise."

Cormac McCarthy
"All the Pretty Horses"

Contents

A Word From The Author

I've been called a dreamer who lives in a fantasy world and suppose I am, for I still believe in fairytales, happy endings, and that elusive prince astride his white horse rescuing the damsel in distress in the nick of time. That is the reason why I wrote this story in a manner that brings glory and reverence in an accurate, yet magical way.

And why not? For fairytales have captured the hearts of the old as well as the young for centuries. There is a piece in all of us: a sliver of innocence left from our youth that comes alive when we read a good feeling story. Many of the movies and plays today are reinventions of old epics and fairy tales. This is because they are surprisingly relevant to real life.

In this book I have resisted my storytelling temptation to invent certain scenic details and dialogue deriving from the horses as texture to this narrative. Dialogue in "bold quotation marks" is conversation and thoughts that are communicated between the equine characters: *Junior, Elena, Emprize Hanover* and *Noble Flirt.* I wrote it this way because I truly believe animals have their own language and communication--- so the bold italic words within is the conversation between the main characters.

The adventures of Junior and Elena are nothing short of a miracle. This real life fairytale delineates Mother Nature's irrefutable power and magic. Hopefully the depth and connotation behind this story will cause a change in human consciousness on how animals feel, think and reason.

The story of Junior and Elena is a an adult fairytale, as adults for the most part are just grown up children who often seek to regress to happier times; and the heartfelt fairytale will often fill the bill.

Junior and Elena is the inspiring tale of a pair of Standardbred racehorses who were thrown together at birth. From the very start both creatures solidified their place in the hearts of Canadians for their story was nationally broadcast to a very approving audience.

Straight out of the Disney fantasy ledger unfolds a modern day fairy tale that people from all walks of life can equally embrace and conclude that *"Dreams do come true."*

Introduction

Throughout centuries there have been numerous books written about horses that captured our attention. Some were about extraordinary racehorses such as Secretariat and Ruffian, and others about a unique horse that possessed a quality and life story that separated them from the average steed.

Almost everyone is familiar with the names *Secretariat, Seabiscuit, Man o' War* and *Dan Patch*. But have you ever heard of a horse named *Beautiful Jim Key?* I'm ashamed to say that having been an avid horse lover, involved in the standardbred industry for 40 years, I had never heard of this exceptional horse.

His name was *"Beautiful Jim Key: The horse that changed the world."* By the time this gelding was eight years old he knew his ABC's, could spell certain words, and even do basic math utilizing numbers up to 30. Hey, that's more than some high school graduates can accomplish!

With the patience of a saint and unconditional love he had for his horse, owner Dr. William Key taught his equine pupil these amazing feats. The doctor did not use a whip or physical tactics to tutor him—he educated only with kindness and patience.

This story illustrates that animals not only have instinct, but they are capable of thinking and even reasoning. Stories like Jim Key's, though rare, can be why the notion of humanlike animal intelligence touches off a powerfully resistive public nerve.

This amazing horse's tale has forever changed the way the world looks at animals. It took a horse with extreme intelligence and a sense of humor to convince a generation of its human responsibility to care for animals proving our inter-connectedness by demonstrating his capability of thoughts and feelings as our own.

Although the story you are about to read may not be as grandiose or riveting as Beautiful Jim Key's, it is the one that is most likely to linger in memory, for more than just awhile.

Junior and Elena: A (Horse) Love Story is both fiction and non-fiction. The protagonists are alive and kicking-- not surprising since they each have four legs. They are two equine athletes that reside in Campbellville, Ontario-- a suburb some 40 miles west of Toronto.

Their story is a magical fusion of reality and fantasy. It is embellished with some fictitious events that have all the makings of a classic Hollywood script—except of course the parts that are factual and ongoing.

There are several parts including the end that is fabricated, for at the time of this writing Junior and Elena were much too young to know if they will even make it to the races. And realistically, the odds of one let alone both competing in the prestigious Canadian Maple Leaf Trot as three-year-olds are insurmountable. But in fairytales-- ANYTHING is possible; thus, I wrote their story as I hope to see it evolve.

In the center of the book is a photo gallery of actual photos of *Elena*, *Junior* and *Emprize Hanover* for your enjoyment. Through these pictures you will re-live the moments and memories of the filly and colt as they grow into amazing athletes.

KEEP DREAMING!

September 2019
Campbelville, Ontario
Mohawk Racetrack

The intermittently fickle Mother Nature had been surprisingly cooperative in Campbellville, Ontario. Saturday, September 7, was a pleasant 75 degrees with but a hint of breeze, and for all intents a picture perfect day for horseracing.

It was the day thousands of horsemen, racing fans, owners and trainers had been anxiously waiting all year for. It was Maple Leaf Day.

Significantly, Maple Leaf Day is when Ontario's finest trotters, both male and female, are on display taking on the best the North American continent has to offer by competing in such prestigious events as *The Peaceful Way, The Wellwood Memorial, The Elegant Image, The Canadian Trotting Classic,* and of course *The Maple Leaf Trot,* a race that is open to all comers.

Maple Leaf Day in Canada is comparable to the Kentucky Derby that is held annually in Louisville, Kentucky for the best equine athletes compete for millions of dollars in purse money, along with the prestigious title.

Race secretary Scott McKelvie did a superb job putting together an outstanding racing card featuring the best trotters the sport has to offer. Headlining todays thirteen-race program is The Canadian Trotting Classic for three-year-olds, and the Maple Leaf Trot for older trotters.

Along with the Trotting Classic and The Maple Leaf Trot is

the Elegant Image—a race where sophomore trotting fillies will compete for almost $500,000---- while freshman trotting fillies will race in the $350,000 William Wellwood Memorial.

Today's race is not much different than the initial inaugural Maple Leaf Trot held in 1950, other than the field of eleven today has some of the finest trotters Mohawk Racetrack has ever seen. And the purse money has escalated from the $5,000 Morris Mite was awarded in 1950 to almost $700,000---of which $350,000 the lucky victor will take home today.

*****

At daybreak, tepid dawning haze peered over the roof of the Mohawk Racetrack grandstand while a ray of sunshine lingered on the infield. Throughout the week leading up to the big day, grooms were seen carrying sloshing buckets to waiting horses in rustling straw-strewn stalls in what is known as 'the detention barn', but politely termed 'the stake's barn.'

Traditionally, equine contenders in major events are isolated in the stakes barn as mandated by the racing commission, as they are ever vigilant to ensure that no horse receives an unfair medicinal advantage.

All week long those that inhabited the Mohawk racing office, plus a handful of Press Box regulars had been buzzing over the possibility that *Peristera* and *Fleetwood*, (formerly known as Elena and Junior) respectively the best three-year-old Ontario sired filly and colt, would disdain entering their respective divisional classics-- The Elegant Image and Canadian Trotting Classic. Instead, both the colt and filly shared by the same owner, Charalamblos Christoforou, but trained in different stables, would be entered in The Maple Leaf.

At first glance that seemed an ambitious undertaking to say the least, but then *Peristera* and *Fleetwood* have overcome virtually insurmountable odds since inception.

Unlike events exclusive to certain age groups, The Maple Leaf Trot has long been carded as a race for three-year-olds and older. Thus, occasionally the younger set had been asked to compete against their elders; though it would seem the "youth" had best be of considerable prowess to attempt such an undertaking.

It was remembered that *In Free*, better known as the dam of *Governor Armbro*, won the Maple Leaf as a three-year-old in 1957, and *Supergrit* did it in 1997-- also at three.

Could *Peristera* and *Fleetwood* be in a league with *In Free* and *Supergrit*? That remains to be seen. But both horses have been ultra impressive versus their age group peers thus far this year as they each have an almost perfect record on the Ontario Gold Circuit.

When interviewed by Dave Briggs for the Globe and Mail, owner Charalamblos Christoforou/aka Mr. C. conceded that stepping up from the Ontario Gold Circuit to the Maple Leaf level is indeed a serious escalation.

"But then I've never owned a colt or a filly like either one of these two before."

He continued, *"Ever since they were foaled it's been one miracle after another, and although one or both may be overmatched, I felt compelled to give them the opportunity. Of course, they'll be racing against each other for the first time and unfortunately only one of them can win—but that'll be up to them, and out of my hands."*

*****

The Maple Leaf Trot was first launched in 1950 at Thorncliffe Park Raceway in Leaside, Ontario, when *Adeline Hanover* and *Morris Mite* finished in a dead-heat after each horse respectively won their division. Since there would be no third heat race-off, a coin toss was done, awarding *Morris Mite* the trophy.

In 1954, The Maple Leaf Trot moved to Old Woodbine and stayed there until 1994 when the race re-located to Woodbine Racetrack where it remained until 2001. For the past 18 years the running of the Maple Leaf Classic has been held as part of Mohawk Raceway's summer stakes extravaganza.

The Maple Leaf Trot is not age restricted and is predominately known for its male champions, but there have been some mares that have won throughout the years--- including the great *Delmonica Hanover* in 1975.

Twelve years later in 1987 it was *Franconia*, then it would be a long 28 years before the unparalleled *Bee A Magician* would "kick the boys to the curb" in 2015.

In that the Maple Leaf is held every year, there have been multiple winners, namely *Tie Silk, No Sex Please, Grandpa Jim* and *San Pail* that have each won the coveted trophy three times. This is a huge feat for just winning it once is commendable, considering the race annually attracts the premier trotters in active racing.

In today's race three-year-old filly *Peristera* will try her luck in adding to the list of these champion mares, but first she will have to beat out ten rather chauvinistic male colts and geldings.

Peristera who will start from post two will be drove by her trainer Jack Moiseyev (Jackie Mo), and if victorious it will be Jackie Mo's second win in the Maple Leaf Trot, having won with *Fools Goal* in 2002.

Chris Christoforou, Jr., trainer/driver for the three-year-old colt *Fleetwood,* has yet to actually bring home a Maple Leaf trophy.

Chris will pilot his 9 to 2 morning line third choice, *Fleetwood.* The colt will leave from post seven.

The remaining field includes: from the rail out, *Musclemania, Peristera, Another Day, Justin Jones, Mr. Muscles, Kadabradabra, Fleetwood, Alwaysagent, Puccio* and *Gravity* is on the extreme outside from post ten. Rounding out the field is *Tomorrowsalock* from post 11, leaving from the second tier.

The morning line favorite is the undefeated four-year-old gelding, Puccio, who set the record for trotting geldings last month in the Cashman Memorial at the Meadowlands. His seasonal earnings approach $1 million.

Second choice is the Muscle Hill four-year-old, Mr. Muscles who has an impressive 8 wins out of 12 starts this year.

Three-year-old *Fleetwood*, the third choice, has come on strongly lately, lowering the famous *Trixton's* 1:50.2 Hambletonian record at The Meadowlands. He has amassed $800,000 plus on his card.

And then there's the lone filly, *Persitera*. It was touch and go all year whether *Peristera* by *E.L.Titan* would even be nominated, as she had been lightly raced at two, having competed in only one baby race which she won handily in 1:56.1. Thereafter, she was stopped after sustaining a minor but nagging injury.

As a three-year-old *Peristera* came back in 2019 with a vengeance and now sports an impressive 3 wins in 5 starts, including a brilliant 1:50.3 tally at Mohawk last month. Thus, owner Christoforou had no second thoughts of supplementing his pride and joy filly for the Maple Leaf Trot.

*****

At 5:30 p.m. sharp the doors opened to the grandstand quickly filling with the usual regulars and more than a smattering of celebrities that were on hand to partake in the big race spectacle and festivities. After all, Maple Leaf night comes but once a year.

Governor David Johnson, pop singer Justin Bieber, comedian Jim Carrey and actor Ryan Gosling---all homebred Canadians and their entourages were there to watch the big race.

You could feel the pulsating excitement that feverishly flowed through the air and the tension among the owners and trainers was so thick you needed the proverbial chef's knife to slice through.

When the national anthem "O Canada" sounded across the loudspeaker, many in the grandstand rose and sang along.

But during the post parade something unexpected happened. While the eleven equine athletes were parading in post-position order, *Peristera* began acting up. Her caretaker, Jamie, rushed to the track to calm the anxious filly, as driver Jackie Mo immediately hopped out of the sulky to assist.

"What's going on with Elena? She never acts like this!" questioned a worried Jackie Mo. *"Is her equipment on right? Is the bit bothering her?"*

As #7, *Fleetwood*, trotted up to *Peristera*, the brown colt planted his hooves and refused to go another step.

"What the hell?" bellowed Chris.

The two horses stood there almost frozen side-by-side

as the filly and colt started nickering. With interlocking eyes *Peristera* produced a blood-curdling whinny as she seemed to be conversing directly to *Fleetwood*. The colt answered back, but in a far more calming tone.

"*Oh my God. They remember each other. I can't believe it!*" stammered Jack.

1

Emprize Hanover Meets Noble Flirt

"You're best friend doesn't have to be human."

Spring 2016
Campbelville
Ontario
Canada

Once upon a time in Campbellville, a community in the geographic township of Nassagaweya in the town of Milton, province of Ontario, a pair of unheralded somewhat innocuous Standardbred mares got thrown together, and thus the story unfolded.

Both mares were owned by standardbred renowned horse trainer, Charalambos "Chris" Christoforou.

Mr. C., as he was affectionately called was a gregarious ethnic Greek in true Zorba style that transplanted to Ontario, Canada, from his birthplace on the Mediterranean island of Cyprus.

In his seasoned years Mr. C. took immense pride in his horses and opted to have them bred to leading Ontario based stallions with aspirations to eventually race their babies. It is every horseman's dream to breed and own the next world champion; but more than the money that can be quite substantial comes the bragging right of owning the next superstar.

Mr. C. had been breeding standardbreds for decades and was

convinced that some actual old-fashioned pure luck was needed, along with intense scientific research.

The ingredients get tossed into a blender--- the DNA and the genetic history--- and then, just *maybe*, you will stumble on that elusive "golden cross."

There is no shortage of tantalizing success stories--- tales of plodding nags who inexplicably foal champions. Although she wasn't a nag, few predicted the dam *Where's The Beach* could throw something like the unparalleled *Somebeachsomewhere?* But it just took one fatal tryst with sire *Mach Three*, and that's exactly what she did.

Where's the Beach a daughter of *Beach Towel* was purchased for $20,000 as a yearling, but never made it to the races. Sensing she may be valuable as a broodmare, her owner bred her to *Mach Three* and that tryst produced one of the greatest pacers in the history of harness racing.

Somebeachsomewhere ranks as one of the best standardbreds to ever look through a bridle. He compelled over $3.2 million in 21 races—winning 20 of them, setting 4 world records including the fastest mile in history of the sport (1:46.4), and recorded sub 1:50 miles in exactly half of his 20 wins.

Of course, his sire and dam have been bred back several times, but nothing approaching *Somebeachsomewhere* has occurred.

But that's horse breeding—a very imprecise science indeed.

*****

It's well known in the standardbred world that most of the time *Overtrick* beat *Meadow Skipper*, but *The Trick* would go on to be considered a failure as a stallion, while his rival *Meadow Skipper* re-wrote the record books and might be the greatest stallion of all time.

In the thoroughbred world conversely, *Affirmed* beat *Alydar* just about every time they ever met, but it was *Alydar* that was the super stud.

Secretariat, said by many to be the greatest thoroughbred to set foot on an American racetrack had the looks and the pedigree to match. But despite possibly having the finest book of mares a first season sire ever covered, *Secretariat* never came close to approaching Canada's *Northern Dancer* in the stallion ranks.

Some thoroughbred breeders utilize figures such as "The Dosage Index," a mathematical figure designed to project the maximum distance the progeny will eventually handle. While others use "The True Nicks" system to gauge which stallions might work best with a given mare.

And then there are those select breeders who simply use their years of experience to decide which stallion they believe will produce a quality foal with their mare.

While horseracing is extremely exciting, it can be heartbreaking, especially when animals don't perform up to expectation. Standardbred racing, also known as harness racing, is often passed down from generations of family members and can be very much a family tradition.

Those enamored with the exciting, yet nerve-wracking lifestyle of racing and horses, tend to be in it for the long run. Once it gets under ones skin it most likely remains indefinitely.

Horses, being barnyard and/or herd animals, are not pets in the conventional sense of the term. However, many owners fall in love with them and treat them like family, despite warnings to the contrary. Breeding and racing is a business and should be handled as such.

But I can personally attest that this is much easier said than done, for having owned hundreds of horses throughout the years-- I have fallen in love with every single one. But that's just me!

Although horses are one of the most regal looking animals-- they are very big, immensely strong and as unpredictable as they are majestic.

Some only think of the glamour involved with horse ownership, but it's not like that for those that work with the animal on a daily basis. Many horsemen and women are literally married to the business-- spending more hours at the barn and with their four-legged family than their two-legged ones.

They don't have the luxury of getting time off as in other careers for they are still needed at the barn on holidays such as Christmas and Easter. Horses need to be cared for each and every one of those 365 days in the calendar year.

This is why most people immersed in the horse business truly love what they do. And that was no different for Mr. C.

One mare owned by Mr. C., *Emprize Hanover* by *Credit Winner,* failed to reach the races. Although she never actually competed, *Emprize* impressed Chris sufficiently in training to breed her first to *Angus Hall,* then to the leading Ontario sire, *Kadabra.* That union resulted with the birth of a beautiful filly that unfortunately died soon after.

Despite losing the *Kadabra* filly, Mr. C. was not ready to give up on this mare so on March 20, 2015 *Emprize Hanover* was bred to *E.L.Titan--* a union that proved successful on the very first attempt.

The second mare, *Noble Flirt,* was sired by the great *Muscle Hill* and was jointly owned by Chris and Irving Storfer of Banjo Farms. Unlike *Emprize, Noble Flirt* did race and accumulated lifetime earnings of $23,830, along with a winning race mark of 1:58.4.

During a brief two-year racing career, *Noble Flirt* made 18 starts with 2 wins, 2 seconds, and 2 thirds. Being a daughter of the great sire *Muscle Hill,* both owners sensed she had more breeding than racing value and chose her first suitor to be the Seelster Farms based, *Holiday Road.*

Noble Flirt was also bred but one time on March 27, 2015, catching immediately. Therefore, given the normal eleven-month gestation period for horses, it figured that *Emprize Hanover* and *Noble Flirt* would foal in close proximity to each other. For that reason, Mr. C. decided to keep the two mares together since they had already become good buddies in pasture prior to insemination.

*****

Situated on Chris's farm was an expansive paddock where all

in-foal and barren mares resided. Most of them being veterans were accustomed to the routine, but *Noble Flirt* somewhat full of herself coming right off the racetrack was about to let the other girls know there was a new gal in town and one bad ass to be reckoned with!

Several of the broodmares were not pleased with this haughty presumptuous newcomer, but *Emprize Hanover* being the senior of the herd embraced the newbie with kindness--- or at least she did once they determined proper rank.

After assorted snorting, kicking, and bucking, the new kid on the block felt she was the victor; but *Emprize,* more seasoned and wiser, didn't give a damn about juvenile appearances having experienced her share of impudent newcomers before. Once the brawling was settled the two became the best of friends.

An introduction of a new horse to an incumbent herd calls for caution as some can be aggressive and occasionally violent, while others are more docile and accepting. Thus when the newcomer seeks entry into an established herd it seems haphazard, yet it's a natural happening that usually doesn't cause much more than passing disruption.

Since the outsider is not the only one affected by the change, the incumbents will redefine their hierarchy to include the stranger. This momentary uncertainty in the social rankings may be the perfect moment for an ambitious young horse to set her position.

Therefore, when Mr. C. would introduce another new mare, *Noble Flirt* kept a protective eye on *Emprize,* not allowing the newbie near her. In return for her friend's comradeship and loyalty, *Emprize* counseled *Noble Flirt* on what to expect as a mother and what it would be like to have her first encounter with the opposite sex.

One day when the two were off from the others, *Noble Flirt* questioned her friend.

"What if I don't like who they're going to breed me to?" nickered *Noble Flirt.* *"What if I'm not attracted to him?"*

"You don't have to worry about that for you'll never see

Holiday Road--- although he is quite a looker. It will all be done by artificial insemination."

"They collect him at the farm, then the vet will simply inject the semen into you," counseled *Emprize.*

"Inject! Oh, no. I hate needles," nickered *Flirt.*

"No. No needles, " laughed Emprize. *"I hate them too. The vet will do it rectally—the procedure will be like your rectal exam."*

"I'm going to be bred to E.L. Titan, who like you is sired by your dad Muscle Hill. If we're lucky we will come into season about the same time, which means we will be inseminated, and if we both catch we will remain together in the same field," further counseled the experienced *Emprize Hanover.*

*****

After the two mares were bred they were transported to nearby High Stakes Farm, a renowned breeding facility owned by Joanne Colville, whose daughter Emma just happened to be the granddaughter of Charalambos "Chris" Christoforou, via his son Chris Jr. -- one of Ontario's leading harness drivers. Thus, Emma was "bred in the purple" for horsemanship, as even at the tender age of thirteen she was already an accomplished equestrian.

High Stakes Farm was one of the more desirable farms in that area to stable a horse for the animal is treated like family. The barns were whitewashed often to hold down disease and feed tubs were disinfected weekly.

Joanne employed only efficient, trustworthy people who truly cared for the horse. Every day the four-legged residents were brought out of their stalls to be brushed and groomed. On extremely cold evenings the horses were blanketed and the stalls were cleaned daily.

Joanne was also one of the more prominent breeders in the area as she too was a horsewoman since birth and functioned as parade marshal at several local racetracks.

She believed in treating horses like children with a combination of love, discipline and patience. But unlike children, horses need custodial care throughout their entire lives—a fact that is sadly ignored by many horsemen.

When someone approached Joanne to purchase one of her four-legged babies she put the prospective buyer through a thorough interrogation.

"Well let me tell you. It's not all fun and games. They're feet are packed with shit. Not just dirt and mud, but real horseshit! Horses are not neat and tidy. They crap all over their stall and stomp on it and every day, you the caretaker must go in there and clean it out."

"It doesn't matter how pretty they are, they're still horses! And unless you understand this and are totally dedicated—this is not for you."

And with that, several of the wanna-be-owners walked away. But those who truly wished to own a horse would learn the procedure and take one home with them as a new member of their family. But it really didn't matter to Joanne if they bought or not, for she would have kept all of the horses if she could.

Upon arriving at High Stakes Farm, *Emprize Hanover* and *Noble Flirt* were assigned the same paddock, although this time *they* were the invaders to the existing herd.

It was springtime and the temperature was slowly moderating. Horses typically prefer early spring to the extremities of hot humid summer or rigid winter.

The grass at High Stakes was now abundant and emerald green. The trees were budding and the flowers were in full bloom. It was the ideal setting for expectant mares to spend the days grazing and preparing for the upcoming duties of motherhood.

Being this was *Noble Flirt's* first attempt as a mom she hadn't anticipated the jerky jabs and spasms that sporadically emerged from her protruding belly. Strangely, the two mares seemed to have developed a language of their own, for when the uncomfortable would occur and *Noble Flirt* would fret, *Emprize* knew exactly how to calm her friend.

"I swear mom these two mares are special. They are unlike any other we have ever had. I believe they talk to each other," Emma informed her mother.

"That's possible. Why shouldn't animals have their own language, as people do?" laughed Joanne.

*****

Feeding time at High Stakes was hectic and a bit chaotic for the equine residents. When the farmhand brought the feed, the mares would not automatically go to their assigned buckets. It was a game played by the horses daily. If one approached her feed tub, *Noble Flirt* would spin and kick, shooing them away—that is, all except for *Emprize*.

In fact, *Noble Flirt* actually allowed her friend to eat from her feed tub as she would go onto the next, making sure the others left *Emprize* alone until she was finished. This is very uncommon for mares usually only share feed with their foals.

During their pregnancy the vet made his usual rounds palpating each mare, assuring all was well with the growing embryos. At the six month check-up he informed Joanne that the foal *Noble Flirt* was carrying seemed rather large for a first time mother. Although this was a bit unusual, he told her it was nothing to worry about.

*****

The next few months flew by. The torrid summer became a bit more tolerant to a welcoming cool fall. Unfortunately, the change of season also meant the frigid Canadian winter was not far behind.

Fall and spring are most appreciated by both man and animal for temperatures are pleasant and the changing autumn leaves can resemble that of a magical Monet painting. Ominously however, Mother Nature is gearing up to show her nasty side.

Winter in Canada is notoriously extreme given the northern latitudes, and caring for the horses has to be managed efficiently. As the days shortened and the air chilled the equines grew long hair to cope with the elements.

It's amazing how nurturing Mother Nature takes over to

protect her four-legged children. When a cold snap would occur the horse "miraculously" appeared fluffier in the morning. Although it seems as if their hair multiplied overnight, it really didn't. The fuller coat is merely the horse's clever way of creating insulation.

However, when the bitter winds became too fierce at the farm, the herd would take refuge in the run-in sheds: protective buildings strategically placed in the center of each paddock. There the mares would find shelter, huddled together to decrease heat loss. That is, all except *Emprize* and *Flirt* who snuggled in a corner, avoiding the others and keeping each other as comfortable as possible.

In her eighth month of pregnancy *Emprize* developed a nagging cough so Joanne immediately started her on a round of antibiotics and watched her closely. *Noble Flirt* sensing something was amiss never left her friend's side.

When *Emprize* went off her food for several days, *Flirt* filled her mouth full with hay and brought it over, dropping it in front of her friend in true nursemaid fashion.

"You have to eat. Remember you are carrying my niece or nephew," Flirt whinnied.

"You need to be strong and healthy so you can keep up with the little one once she or he arrives."

*****

Finally, the wrath of winter subsided and the snow began melting as temperatures climbed to the high-thirties during the day.

It was Monday night, February 29th (leap year no less) when Emma noticed *Emprize* acting uncomfortably. The mare was immediately placed in a large foaling stall in the breeding barn. Once separated, *Noble Flirt* still in the paddock paced the fence. Hearing her friend's distress call, *Emprize* nickered back. It was obvious the two mares were highly agitated at being separated.

"Mom, Flirt and Emprize are having an anxiety attack from being

separated. We better bring Flirt in the barn and stall her next to Emprize before one of them gets hurt," Emma said.

Once in adjoining stalls and visible to each other, the two mares calmed down, quietly communicating in a language that no human could decipher.

"I think it's almost time," whispered *Emprize* through the bars.

"Oh, I'm so scared. I wish I could be in there to help you," Noble Flirt replied, although she had no knowledge of what was about to transpire.

*****

It would be a long drawn out four days before *Emprize* would deliver her foal. On March 4, she dropped a healthy bay filly with a small white star on her forehead.

Luckily, the new mother had no complications during the birthing process, as she hadn't in her previous deliveries.

The newborn was quite a looker. She was tall with long legs and possessed a white splash across her forehead. She was a real beauty who had a bit of noticeable spunk. With no visible abnormalities apparent, Joanne was quite pleased with the filly.

Of course there isn't much you can tell about the aspirations of a newborn foal. There's no way to measure heart and competitive desire. There's no way to tell if the foal hit the genetic lottery—drawing on all that is quick and efficient in the gene pool.

Being in the business for decades Joanne knew only too well that those answers would come later.

After several minutes the newborn stood somewhat wobbly and began nursing. As if needing her friends' approval, *Emprize* nudged the unsteady filly to where *Noble Flirt* could see and smell her. After sniffing the foal through the stall bars, *Noble Flirt* let out a loud whinny, informing *Emprize* what a nice filly she had.

"That's a fine looking little girl."

"She is so pretty. I hope my foal looks like her," Flirt neighed.

The newborn, startled at the sudden loud snorts, cowered behind her mom for protection and continued nursing. After she was done feeding the satisfied foal stretched out in the thick bed of straw and promptly dozed off. *Emprize*, relieved that the ordeal was over and her job was successfully accomplished, resumed munching the alfalfa hay.

2

A Complicated Delivery

"All horses deserve at least once in their lives to be loved by a little girl."

March 4, 2016
High Stakes Farm
Moffat

The day after *Emprize* delivered her foal, Mr. C., the proud owner, visited the new addition to his stable and was pleasantly surprised.

"I think we got the best that Emprize and E. L. Titan had to offer. Looks like a there's a good cross here, Joanne," said the happy Greek.

"I agree, but you know as well as I do, Chris, that anything can happen between now and when they make it to the races," Joanne said matter-of-factly.

The next several weeks, *Mama Emprize*, her unnamed filly, and *Noble Flirt* were turned out together in the same paddock where they frolicked and interacted as a family.

Although *Emprize's* filly was average size, she was exceptionally strong and athletic. It didn't take the young one long to realize the natural dance movement that is part of the genetic gift and soon trotted with the speed and finesse her mother possessed.

When *Emprize* needed a break from mothering duties, *Aunt Noble* would assume the duty of baby-sitter. After several hours of grazing and light exercise Emma would lead the trio to the barn for the night, always placing the two mares in adjoining stalls.

One evening Emma noticed that *Noble Flirt* seemed to be in discomfort. The very pregnant first time mama was anxiously pacing the stall-- ears pinned back, tail swishing and biting at her protruding belly.

Upon examination the vet told Joanne that *Noble Flirt* was in the early stages of delivery. Since this was new to her and *Flirt* didn't quite fathom what was happening, she became apprehensive.

After the veterinarian left, *Noble Emprize* seemed to relax a bit, allowing Emma and Joanne to grab a hasty dinner for they both sensed there could be some anxious hours ahead.

"I'm really scared. I didn't expect it to feel like this," Flirt told *Emprize*.

"Just try to relax. It's your first time and it is a bit frightening, but I'm sure everything will be okay."

"Pretty soon my little girl will have a cousin to play with," *Emprize* snorted as she curled her lip.

"I'm right here next door so I'll be able to keep an eye on you. I won't rest until your little one is here with us."

*****

Back in the house Emma and Joanne grabbed a quick shower and made a sandwich.

"You know mom, it's really strange but Noble Flirt seems to be in more distress than our other broodmares prior to foaling. Do you think there is a problem?" Emma asked.

"Probably not. But being it is her first we better watch her carefully," Joanne answered.

*****

As the labor pains intensified, *Noble Flirt* frantically paced the stall pausing intermittently to lie down, though not for long. Her incessant whimpers resembled the wail of a female in labor.

Emprize Hanover sensing her friends' anxiety and pain assured her through soothing whispers, *"Hang in there, Noble. I know help will be here soon."*

After finishing eating an exhausted Emma had barely closed her eyes when she was awoken by persistent shrieks emanating from the barn area and immediately woke her mother for she sensed trouble.

Upon entering the barn the air was filled with an eerie silence. The usual meowing of kittens was mute and the boisterous barn dogs were huddled together in the corner. If a needle had dropped on the frozen barn floor, it could be heard loud and clear.

As Emma and Joanne approached the breeding stall the overpowering smell of equine amniotic fluid was evident.

"I think something is wrong, mom. It's just too quiet considering the ruckus we heard before," Emma said as she turned on the light switch.

From inside the walls of *Noble Flirt's* cubicle came a faint sound that mirrored a newborns whimper. Next door in *Emprize's* stall the loud, distressed cries resumed. Rushing over, Joanne observed *Emprize* frantically pacing from one end to the other with her little one at her flank. It was obvious the two were distressed.

As she approached *Noble Flirt's* stall Emma stopped in her tracks for this wasn't what she expected to see. Lying in the middle of the stall floor was a barely moving newborn foal. The colt was still attached by the umbilical cord to his almost motionless mother.

"Mom, hurry! Come quick. I think something is wrong with Flirt."

When Joanne observed the mare, instinctively she knew it was too late. Sprawled out in the thick bed of straw was *Noble Flirt*, engulfed by a rising pool of blood. The mare was desperately gasping for air. It was obvious she had severely hemorrhaged during delivery.

Joanne told Emma to fetch some colostrum from the cooler for time was crucial and if the newborn foal didn't get the special milk soon he could die.

When Emma came back with the colostrum she immediately administered it to the colt while Joanne vainly tended to the fallen mare.

"Mom, what are we going to do?" Emma cried. *"There are no surrogate mares available for the colt and he'll die if we don't do something soon."*

*****

"Those chilling words echoed through the barn, reaching my ears, then melted around me like something out of a sci-fi-movie".

"She's talking about me," thought *Noble Flirt.*

"Although I knew that the voice was real-- coming from the young girl who had taken such good care of me-- it seemed so surreal at that moment".

"I looked over and through blurry vision I saw the most beautiful foal-- looking helplessly at me with frightened eyes."

"I can't die! I have a son that needs me."

"Growing weaker by the minute I knew my time was running out. I could barely get the words out, " Emprize, you must take care of my son."

"I can't leave this world until I know my baby boy is cared for, and Emprize, you are the only one I trust to raise him."

*****

As *Noble Flirt* took her final breath, Joanne went over to the foal. She cut the umbilical cord and covered him with a heated blanket while Emma resumed administering the colostrum.

Peering through the stall bars was a helpless and distraught *Emprize Hanover* as she watched her friend lying there motionless. At that exact moment Emprize let out a loud squeal and to everyone's surprise the colt called back.

"With my dying breath I let Emprize know how much I loved her and begged her to take care of my son as if he were her own."

"I know she heard and understood me, even though my voice

was but a whisper now, because she called out to my foal and I heard him answer back. Knowing that he would be cared for and loved, I left this world".

*****

Anxiously awaiting the vet's arrival, Joanne went to fetch more heated blankets. As Emma watched over the colt, she was inspired by what would be a brilliant brainstorm.

When Joanne returned with the blankets she was stunned to see her daughter carefully toting the newborn swaddled in a blanket over to *Emprize's* stall.

On average a newborn foal weighs approximately 10 percent of their mothers weight at birth. *Noble Flirts* colt was a big boy, weighing in about 120 pounds.

Luckily, Emma was athletic and in great shape, so she was capable of transporting the colt from stall to stall on her own. The astute young woman enwrapped the foal in a blanket, gathered both ends and securely positioned him in the middle. With adrenaline soaring and the willpower and desire to save the young colt, Emma proceeded.

"Emma, I don't know if that's a good idea. Emprize might hurt the foal. Mares don't usually accept another's newborn. I've never had a broodmare with her young one by her side accept another's. It takes a very specific temperament from the mare and I'm not sure how Emprize will react."

"But mom I HAVE to try. Emprize knows this is Noble Flirts colt and she won't hurt him. And he doesn't have Noble Flirts scent on him because she was never near him."

As the commotion increased, *Emprize's* filly grew anxious and a tad bit irritated as she watched another foal invade *her* home. The nervous filly scurried over to her mother who quickly assured her all was okay.

Joanne and Emma watched somewhat awestruck as *Emprize Hanover* slowly made her way over to the shivering colt lying on the floor and began cleaning his sticky face with her warm, soft tongue.

The mare continued washing the foal until all of the afterbirth was gone. Closing his eyes, the colt started making soft noises.

Emprize and *Noble Flirt's* foal seemed to be conversing with one another; producing strange sounds only they seemed to understand. After several unsuccessful attempts to stand, Emma helped the colt up on his four wobbly legs, and like a typical drunkard, he wobbled over to *Emprize* and began nursing.

"*Look. He's nursing! She's letting him nurse!*" Emma screamed.

"*Well I'll be. She's accepted the colt as her own. And look—Emprize's filly is nursing the other side.*"

As she wiped the tears streaming down her face Emma took out her I-Phone and snapped several pictures. A few minutes later the veterinarian arrived and was stunned to see the three horses together in the stall.

"*I can't believe what I'm seeing. In my 40 years of practice I've never observed this. This is a miracle, that's for sure,*" the vet said incredulously.

"*Emprize realized this colt belonged to Noble Flirt and she loved her friend so much that she intuitively knew what she was doing was right. She totally grasped the situation and through her body language and maternal nurturing she telegraphed, "I get it. I know what you need me to do. I've got this,*" Joanne replied.

"*This truly is remarkable for this scenario won't work with most mares. It takes a very specific temperament and acceptance from the mare which is very rare,*" the vet told Joanne.

"*Emprize is doing her job and doing it quite well I must say,*" he continued.

"*Now you two have to be onboard as well for this is going to require a strict regimen of administering the hormones at the right time in order to keep the mare lactating. She is not only feeding one hungry mouth, but now two.*"

"*This is a very uncommon situation and I have to be honest with you—the colt is not out of danger yet! There's a 50/50 chance he will survive!*"

"*No worries, doc. I'm sure my daughter and I can do this. The good Lord doesn't give you more than you can handle. This is a very, very special foal and we will make sure he and his little sister get the best care,"* Joanne assured the veterinarian.

As the vet and his two assistants removed *Noble Flirt's* body from her stall, Emma detected a tear fall from *Emprize's* eye in despondent fashion as she continued nursing both foals.

3

A Brother From Another Mother

"If God created anything more beautiful then a horse, he kept it for himself."

Fall 2016
High Stakes Farm
Moffat

The season of spring in Canada can be a magical time for the air is clean and fragrant and the temperatures slowly begin to rise. The blooming flowers are portrayed in vivid Technicolor, the fields are covered with garland chrysanthemum, and cherry trees flaunt almost magenta-like blossoms.

Spring is known as "the season of renewal of life," for both plants and animals are being born. After digging out from under mounds of snow, the season is welcomed and embraced by the human and animal inhabitants of the region. It is also the time for many festivities such as the Maple Syrup Festival. At the festival one has the opportunity to learn how sweet syrup is made and to enjoy the wonderful flavors of tasty maple products.

It was a typically hectic time at High Stakes Farm, for there was so much work that had to be done. Fences had to be mended following winters' onslaught and the individual fields needed to to be tended to as well. In addition, Joanne was busy making all the preparations for the resident mares to be bred to the years selected suitors.

Although everyone was relieved of having endured another brutal winter it wasn't the same at High Stakes without *Noble Flirt's* presence. *Emprize* was busy tending to her two foals but it was obvious she missed her friend. The two mares had developed an unusual unique bond, being virtually inseparable for over a year—similar in some ways to the connection that is shared by twin embryos within a mother's womb. It's an affiliation so strong and powerful that neither time nor distance can shake.

Emprize had been looking forward to raising her new foal with *Flirt* and her little one, but she now had the difficult and lonely task of bringing up not one, but two foals on her own.

Being a veteran *Emprize* knew what to expect with one little one, but sensed two could be a tad overwhelming. With two foals there definitely could be double trouble; thus an overprotective mother could never let her guard down for more than an instant.

There's an abundance of mischief a young foal, like small children can get into. In addition, some broodmares can get nasty and aggressive to other mares foals and will kick them when they get too close. Then there is the normal frisky play that occurs between colts and fillies that at times can be problematic.

Emprize recalled the horrific incident that happened the year before. She witnessed several fillies playing together when one accidentally got kicked in the leg shattering it beyond repair and sadly had to be euthanized. *Emprize* couldn't bear to have that happen to one of hers. She would just die if anything happened to one of her kids. It was agonizing enough losing her best friend. No, now she had to pay extra attention to these two.

Furthermore, she promised *Noble Flirt* she would take care of her son, and if it were the last thing she ever did she would not break the vow she made to her dying friend.

*****

One day when Emma and Joanne were admiring the two

youngsters as they romped in the field the girl said, *"I think it's time we named Emprize Hanover's foals."*

For horse owners, naming your foal is one of the most exciting things about owning one. The way of naming a standardbred racehorse is a process steeped in tradition and protocol.

Typically, an owner will select a name that pays homage to the foal's lineage, while perhaps reflecting its individuality. It can be something pertaining to its owner's name, or it may be about the foal's appearance.

Some people like to name their foals after famous songs and some after celebrities. But when you choose a name of a famous person, you must first get written approval from them to be able to use it.

The great Thoroughbred champion *Nyquist,* was named by owner J. Paul Reddam after Gustav Nyquist—a winger for Reddam's beloved Detroit Wings.

And then there's *Man o' War*----perhaps the greatest thoroughbred racehorse of all times who was named by his owner in honor of her husband, August Belmont Jr. after he joined the U. S. Army at the ripe age of 65.

Although naming your horse is almost as exciting as naming your child, there is a lot of time and thought that goes into this process.

After several minutes of thinking Emma said, *"Let's call them Junior and Elena for now."*

"I like that. He looks like a Junior and Elena is a pretty name. That's it. It's Junior and Elena," Joanne replied. *"But when they get ready to race we will have to give them their official registered race names."*

"But I'm really worried about Emprize. She looks so sad without her friend, Noble Flirt."

"I know, but I think her two kids will keep her so busy that she will have no time for significant mourning" her daughter replied.

*****

It took awhile, but after several weeks Elena finally accepted her brother from another mother. After all, it happened so fast she didn't have time to distinguish the privilege of being an only child to sharing her mother with a colt, no less. But even if she had, there wasn't much she could do about it now.

Elena recalled that night when Emma brought the trembling foal wrapped in a blanket into *her* home and placed him at *her* mother's hooves. *Emprize*, being a kind and compassionate mare, accepted the little one and took him in as her own.

But wasn't this Aunt *Flirt's* foal? What ever happened to her? All she remembered was hearing some kind of ruckus taking place in her stall, and then two people removing something covered in a blanket, and she never saw her Aunt again. Now her mother seemed sad all the time. She didn't know why, for she had not one, but two beautiful kids to call her own—although one would have certainly been enough!

Elena *tried* to be kind to her adopted brother but sometimes he was just too much of a pest. Whenever she would try to enjoy quality 'mother/daughter' time with her mom, that little brat would always ruin it. He would come trotting over and start to nurse on the other side.

"Of course, mom wouldn't stop him. So there we were, two growing foals nursing off MY mother. Every once in awhile we would get a little frisky and tug too hard at her teets, thus mom would give us a good one by biting us on our bottoms."

"I guess you can say that between the two of us, I am the more independent one. My little brother is a mommy's boy— always up her butt."

"It's really kind of disgusting. I mean A BOY following his mama around, instead of letting ME—her princess-- having some one-on-one time."

"I know you probably think I'm just being selfish."

"I'm not jealous, I just didn't ask for this. I don't know what it's like to have 'my' mom all to myself and I suppose I never will, so I might as well make the best of it."

"Yep, I guess that brat is here to stay!"

*****

"*Okay. Little Miss Priss told her side, now it's time to tell you MY side of the story,*" Junior neighed.

"*And THIS is the TRUE STORY!*"

"*All I remember is one minute feeling warm and safe, and the next lying in a dark damp stall, shivering and trembling. I had no idea what I was supposed to experience, but being cold, alone, and scared didn't seem right!*"

"*I cried out for my mom, but nothing happened. Then I saw a big beautiful creature lying on the ground near me, but she was barely moving. At first she tried to make some noises, but then she stopped.*"

"*I knew this was my mom for she was looking at me with big beautiful, loving brown eyes; but they were so sad looking.*"

"*Then I heard a woman's soothing voice telling me everything was going to be alright, and someone wrapping me in a fuzzy blanket and lifting me up.*"

"*The next thing I remember is having my face and body washed by a warm, wet tongue, and then an awe-inspiring feeling came over me that I was truly loved.*"

"*I tried to stand on my legs but was too weak and kept falling. The nice girl that wrapped me in a blanket helped me up and guided me over to this mare who would become my new mom.*"

"*But as I began nursing I felt a sharp nip on my rump which made me jump. When I looked, I saw another foal standing there staring at me giving me a nasty look.*"

"*Well, mom gave her hell for biting me and then that little insolent pest FINALLY left me alone.*"

"*I don't know why this nuisance is always there, taking time away from me and 'my' mom, but I guess she's not leaving.*"

"*Oh well, I guess if you can't beat 'em, you gotta join 'em.'*"

"*I suppose I better make the best of it and try to get along with this pain-in-the-neck, for I don't want mom to be mad at me. After all--- I KNOW I'm her favorite!*"

*****

It's general practice that when mares give birth, dams with fillies are generally separated from the dams with colts. But in the case of *Emprize Hanover*, the mare and her two foals were turned out in a field by themselves, away from the others.

As the sister and brother grew and became more confident and independent, they began leaving their mom more to play with one another. It was a sight that would put a smile on a sad sacks face for the two young ones would chase each other, bucking and kicking, but making sure they never hurt the other.

Emprize got more comfortable with the idea that her daughter and adopted son had actually accepted one another and at times even looked like they liked each other.

But even though her two babies got along, they still competed for her attention—especially at feeding time. When one of them would nurse, the other would trot over and nurse on the other side.

Poor *Emprize*! Although she was quite sore from all the tugging and biting on her teats, she never once denied her babies.

During the evening the three horses were left outside because the weather was so pleasant. It was their favorite time of day for the flies were absent and the temperature was perfect.

The run-in-shed always provided a thick, clean bed of straw for them to rest in. *Mama* would go on one side to keep an eye on her kids while Junior and Elena would go to the other, lying close to one another. Sometimes the two young horses slept with their necks intertwined. They seemed to always be touching one another in some way.

As the days passed by the two foals that were brought together in a time of heartache were growing unusually close to one another. The weanlings seemed to have developed that special unique bond that their mothers once shared.

No matter how much Elena irritated her brother all she had to do was bat her big, brown eyes and he melted. There's no doubt that Junior was smitten with his pretty sister.

*****

"You know, I'm glad my mom took you in as my brother. At first I didn't like it, but now you are my best friend," Elena nickered.

"The only regret I have is I wish I had known my 'real' mom, at least for a little bit. But our mom is the best mom in the world. And you know something, you're the best sister," said Junior as he licked Elena's face.

"And I have to tell you a secret, Elena. You had me at the first whinny. I might have acted hard to get, but you won my heart right from the beginning."

Watching her filly and colt nuzzling together, *Emprize* had a warm and peaceful feeling. As the two young horses caressed each other's necks it brought back memories of when Noble Flirt would do that to her. It seemed her friend always knew when she needed a little loving and attention.

Emprize looked up at the star lit sky, recalling the first time she laid eyes on *Noble Flirt*.

Noble Flirt was a real looker. She was a beautiful bay mare with a head of exquisite turn. Her eyes were unusually large, shaped like a doe's, half hidden by the thick forelock and her perked ears were well sloped forward.

When *Noble Flirt* was initially turned out amongst the other broodmares she spotted *Emprize* first and trotted over to her with nostrils open and upper lip in motion.

"Who are you?" the recent retiree asked.

"My name is Emprize Hanover and you are now on my turf."

And that was the beginning of a beautiful and loving friendship.

"I know you are up there watching, Flirt. I miss you terribly and hope to make you proud of us. Your son who is now named Junior is a fine young colt who reminds me of you in many ways."

"He has your big almond shaped eyes, and every time I look at them I remember all the wonderful times we shared."

"I promised to care of him as my own and I am doing the best I can, for I truly love him with all my heart, for he is you,

all over again! You were like a sister to me and I will never love another as I do you."

"I treasure the happy times we had and I sense that someday once again we will be together, running and romping beyond the Rainbow Bridge."

4

That Dreaded Weaning Time

"A weaning baby that does not cry aloud will die on its mothers back."

October, 2016
Moffat, Ontario

Being herd animals, horses often bluff, exaggerate, ignore, maintain alliances, betray loyalties, reward good deeds, seek affection and generally thrive better in unison rather then solidarity.

Weaning or separating a young colt or filly from his dam is one of the most traumatic situations a horse will endure. It can be equally heart wrenching for the human that is assigned to the unpleasant task.

On most breeding farms weaning generally happens at about six months of age. The youngsters are gradually introduced to a new diet, a new environment, and will have to quickly adjust to new rules of social organization.

Breaking that strong 'mother-foal' bond is always heart wrenching, but in captivity it's necessary. Having spent the first five or six months by their dam's side receiving the nutritional requirement is met solely from the mare's milk. Foals experiment and begin nibbling small amounts of grain from their dam's buckets within weeks of birth and will consume more substantial amounts by the time they're two to three months of age.

In the wild mares wean their foals on their own and when they are ready. It's not uncommon for the previous foal to linger until the new foal arrives. Feral mares are virtually almost always pregnant as the alpha stallion re-breeds his ladies as soon as they come back in heat following foaling.

Some barren mares might permit offspring to linger till nearly two years of age, but on the average domesticated foals get weaned by six months or thereabouts, regardless of the mother's current pregnancy status. This is standard procedure at most breeding establishments.

High Stakes Farm, like most other breeding farms practices interval weaning. Initially, the mares with the oldest foals get separated first; generally when the young ones are occupied with each other. The mares are then turned out with their normal resident group, but out of sight and earshot from the babies.

This method has been proven to have the least stress on foals, as most will quickly adjust to their normal buddies, although they will now be separated by sex. But this was not the case with Elena and Junior, for neither was ever in contact with any other youngsters. All they ever knew was one another and their mother, *Emprize Hanover.*

"How are we going to do this mom? Elena and Junior are so attached to each other and have never been with any other colts or fillies," Emma asked Joanne.

"It's not going, to be easy but it has to be done. Unfortunately, Elena and Junior are not the same sex so they cannot stay together indefinitely. In fact, we have left them together too long already."

"They are almost seven months old and Junior is becoming adolescently studdish. We can't have any inadvertent mistakes occur here. And being that Emprize is back in foal to Cornaro Dasolo, she needs to stop nursing and milking."

"Both Junior and Elena are healthy, strong, and fairly independent. I think it's going to be harder on Junior, though, " Joanne said. *"He's definitely a mommy's boy."*

"It will also be tough on Emprize for she is by far one of the best mothers we have ever had. She is so dedicated and loves those two unconditionally."

"I think it would be best for everyone if we bring Emprize back to your grandpa's farm where she will be out with other pregnant mares. This way the three will be miles apart and will not hear the others cry out."

*****

Ever since the birth of Junior the local media dubbed Elena and Junior "a special pair of horses." They were the new stars of the area and people across the country followed their story closely. Their unconventional story brought throngs of curious people to High Stakes Farm to witness these equine celebrities; thus, were handled by humans far more than the other foals.

Therefore by the time *Emprize's* two kids were separated they were more amenable to people than perhaps their equine peers. Concerned about the upcoming separation process Joanne invited a few close friends over to interact with Elena and Junior to keep them occupied while she and Emma removed *Emprize* from the field.

While Elena was enjoying the extra attention, clingy Junior initially refused to leave his mama's side. He was a rather intuitive colt with extra smarts and knew something was about to happen that he wouldn't like.

As Elena nuzzled up to several young children, Junior refrained, pinning his ears back, turning his back to his fans telegraphing he might throw a kick if they got too close.

Finally, Emma distracted him sufficiently for Joanne to lead *Emprize* out of the paddock and onto the waiting trailer. All was going well until the colt realized *Emprize* was no longer there. As the trailer exited the driveway Junior let out a bloodcurdling scream.

"Elena. Hurry. Come quick! Something is happening. They are taking our mother away!" he bellowed as he charged the gate with his tail cocked high and nostrils flaring.

Being the more sensible one, Elena trotted over to her brother and placated him. Although somewhat confused, both brother and sister temporarily succumbed to the lure of carrots and apples that were being offered by their obliging fans.

When Joanne returned to High Stakes she told Emma, *"I know Emprize was sad to leave her children but I think she was a little relieved to be able to rest now. After all, the weaning process is familiar to her and she must prepare for her new little one who will arrive in the spring."*

"But I think it's best if we leave Junior and Elena together a few more weeks before we separate them, to get them gradually used to the idea of being without one another."

"I agree. We don't want to stress them out too much at once," Emma said.

*****

For the next two weeks the filly and her brother remained together. During the first few days after weaning, occasionally they would whinny and look for *Emprize*, but by the end of the week had settled down and seemed to have accepted the new situation.

Over at Chris Christoforou's farm, *Emprize* was adjusting to a life without her kids. Although she often thought about them she was assured they would be taken care of.

After all it had been difficult and stressful having to nurse and watch over two foals. Now she could get some well-needed rest before bringing another foal into the world.

Sometimes at night when she would get lonely, *Emprize* would gaze at the moonlit sky and imagine seeing *Noble Flirt* trotting among the clouds. After a hard rain would occur and a rainbow appeared in the sky, *Emprize* visualized The Rainbow Bridge with *Noble Flirt* standing on it waiting for her.

There were several times when she thought she heard *Flirt* call out, only to discover it was one of the neighboring broodmares. Although she tried to bond with some of the others, she knew she would never again experience that special friendship she once shared with *Noble Flirt*.

*****

Several weeks after weaning, subsequently Joanne and Emma knew the unpleasant time had come. It was inevitable that Elena and Junior had to be separated and placed with members of their own sex and approximate age.

It was a cloudy, brisk day in early November when the early chapters of this remarkable story would turn the page as Elena and Junior must now go their separate ways. It would be a frightening and uncertain voyage as they commenced a new life on their own.

What lies ahead for the bay filly with a white star and her adopted brother? No one knows for sure, but for Junior and Elena it is now time for advanced adolescence and the magic of a new beginning.

5

A New Chapter: On Their Own

"He's of the color of the nutmeg. And the heat of the ginger...he is pure air and fire; and the dull elements of earth and water never appear in him, but only in patient stillness while his rider mounts; he is indeed a horse and all the other jades you may call beasts."

Fall 2016
High Stakes Farm

ELENA

For Elena, life without her mother and brother was crestfallen and lonely. Initially, the first few weeks in the weanling field out with the other yearling fillies, was a bit intimidating and overwhelming, as she had only previously associated with her immediate family.

It is common practice that young horses will pair in twos, practicing the buddy system. In this particular herd there was a total of 12 fillies, which theoretically would be six sets of two. Instead, there were four pairs of two fillies and one group of three. And then there was Elena.

It's not because the others ignored her-- she just wouldn't warm up to them, so for the first two months of being separated from her family, Elena went solo.

Although Joanne and Emma were concerned about the filly's solitary, Elena appeared to like being on her own. She had always been the independent one and the alpha, but at least then she had another to play and cavort with.

It's unhealthy for a young horse not to interact and socialize with other horses. But when two horses become so attached that any form of separation leads to stress verging on panic, the virtues of companionship are outweighed by the complications it brings.

This was the case with Elena and Junior.

While most horses will work out their peer differences without human intervention, it's still important to be aware of what's going on.

Whenever another filly approached Elena, she would quickly shoo away the wanna-be friend. Eventually the others stopped trying to befriend her and went off on their own.

*****

"I miss you Junior. I know you were a pest, but I would do anything to have you with me again. I hope you are okay."

"And mama, I miss you so much. I was mad at you for bringing another foal into our family, but now I know why you did."

"You loved Aunt Noble so much and would do anything for her. Raising her son was the most compassionate and unselfish thing anyone could do."

"I'm so proud of you and pray that someday we will all be with each other again."

Several weeks after the brother and sister were separated, Elena thought she heard a familiar sound afar. It sounded like her little brother's voice.

She called back and ran the field looking for him, but he wasn't there. With her head hung down, she solemnly trotted to the run-in shed—far away from the other fillies.

<u>JUNIOR</u>

Being with strange new colts took some time for Junior to adjust. He was by far the least aggressive and perhaps even the most subservient in the group of ten colts. In the beginning the other colts would try to play with Junior, although they were a bit too rough. He would turn his back and trot away, not wanting any trouble.

One day Junior befriended a black colt named Sammy. Being of similar temperament the two colts hit it off and stayed pretty much to themselves, avoiding any confrontations with the others.

Although Sammy was really nice, he couldn't replace his sister, Elena. She was certainly a pain, but he really missed her and would do anything to see her again.

Of course he longed to see his mother, but surprisingly he found he missed his sister more. Elena had always watched out for him and made sure he didn't get into any trouble. She was his rock, and now she was gone!

He wondered why they had to separate him and Elena from their dam. Why couldn't they all live together forever? Didn't he suffer enough by losing his real mom, without ever having known her?

He heard Joanne and Emma occasionally talk about *Noble Flirt* and from what he gathered his real mom was a smart, beautiful mare that was attached to his "surrogate" mom, *Emprize*.

"I wish I could see you, Elena. I wouldn't be a brat anymore. I promise I will be a better brother."

"Why can't we be together? They said it is because I am a boy and you are a girl that we had to separate, but we were together for a long time and did just fine."

"And Mama Emprize, I want to thank you for taking me in. It had to be difficult raising another's baby while you had one of your own!"

"I know I was a pest following you around all the time, but I was afraid of losing another mother."

"Did I do something to make them take me away from you and my sister? If I did, I'm sorry."

Sensing his friend's anguish, Sammy went over to Junior and began caressing his neck. Returning the favor, Junior nuzzled him back as he thought to himself, *"You are a good friend, Sammy, but you will never be my Elena."*

<u>EMPRIZE HANOVER</u>

Learning to live without her two kids was much more difficult than *Emprize Hanover* ever imagined. It had never been this hard before when she was weaned from her other foals. Having had three previous kids you would have thought she was used to the routine, but for some reason these two were special---so very special.

She found herself often thinking about those two and her heart ached.

Of course her daughter, Elena, was wonderful. She was a beautiful filly who was independent and never gave her a bit of trouble. Then one day a few weeks after giving birth to her filly, her best friend *Noble Flirt* unexpectedly died.

She heard commotion coming from her stall and knew something terrible was wrong. Although she couldn't get in to help her, she tried comforting her.

"I was horrified to find out she was in serious trouble and wasn't going to survive. I heard Noble Flirt call out and ask me to take her son and raise him as my own."

"I assured her I would. I would do anything for her, for she was the sister I never had. Her son is the sweetest thing and I'm proud to call him mine."

"Although my daughter was extremely agitated in the beginning, she eventually warmed up and became the best big sister. I hope they are both doing well. I have to believe that someday I will see them again."

"No matter how many other foals I may have, those two will always be my favorites and live in my heart."

"My deepest wish is that they both grow up to be healthy and happy and have great forever homes."

6

Junior heads to Florida

"Horses are the dolphins of the plains, the spirits of the wind; yet we sit astride them for the sake of being well-groomed, whereas they could have all the desire in the world to bolt, but instead, they adjust their speed and grace, only to please us, never to displease."

November, 2017
Sunshine Meadows Training Center
Delray Beach, Florida

After they were weaned and separated, Junior and Elena spent the next several months grazing in the sparing green grass, developing into healthy, happy yearlings.

Although colts are normally larger than fillies, Elena was a good size, with a well-rounded rump and broad, strong shoulders.

Junior was average size and an extremely handsome colt. Joanne had stated that she had never seen a colt as striking as he was. He was almost filly-like for he was much finer boned than the other yearling colts on the farm.

He had a unique Arabian-like head with a long, silky mane and the most beautiful almond shaped brown eyes—just like his mother, *Noble Flirt*. However, his temperament was more like his adopted mom, *Emprize*, who was laid back and docile.

Owner Charamblos Christoforou aka/Mr. C. decided to send

the colt with his son, Chris Jr., to South Florida to be broke and conditioned at Sunshine Meadows Training Center located in Delray Beach, Florida.

Mr. C. was very proud of his son, Chris Jr., for he was an accomplished standardbred trainer and driver in Canada.

Elena would be under the care of Joanne's fiancée, Jack Moiseyev, also a renowned trainer-driver who was stabled at First Line Training Center in nearby Campbellville.

Jack also grew up in the business. His father Sid, was a successful horseman at the New York and New Jersey racetracks. Like his father, Jack was an energetic, elliptical talker who had many stories to tell.

During his career, Jackie Mo, as he was known, had set several world records in the United States with both trotters and pacers, and was one of the more sought out harness drivers in the business.

*****

Aboard the southern bound horse van were ten anxious fillies and colts, including Sammy and Junior. While boarding, Junior thought he spotted Elena in a nearby field amongst other fillies. Although it had been a few months since he had been with her, he would know that face anywhere.

And the way she moved! Elena had a unique way of trotting; holding her tail high and a wiggle that he'd come to cherish.

After the attendant backed Junior into his allotted space in the trailer, the colt got a better look and was positive it WAS his sister. He called out to her and to his surprise, she answered.

When Elena heard her brothers call, she trotted as fast as she could to the fence line, tail cocked high and ears forward as she threw her head.

Boy, had she grown! She appeared much taller than he remembered, but she still was and always will be his little sister who he loved more than anything in the world!

Standing at the fence Elena bellowed, *"It's so good to see you, Junior. I miss you so."*

"Where are you going? You just got here. Please don't leave me again!"

But before he could answer, the doors to the van closed tight and the trailer exited the driveway as it headed down the winding road. Again, Junior bellowed and Elena responded--- until they could no longer hear one another.

Sensing that his friend was distraught, Sammy who was in the next stall stretched his head around and sniffed his nose, but Junior, too devastated to leave his sister once again, stood there oblivious to him.

*****

The trip from Ontario to Delray Beach, Florida, was a tedious and somewhat grueling 1,500 miles. The first night the van stopped half way at Pinehurst, North Carolina, to let the horses off to rest.

Early into the second day the mild weather turned nasty and it began to rain heavily. As the water plummeted down on the metal roof of the trailer it made a loud noise causing several of the yearlings to get spooked.

The attendees in the trailer immediately went to them, soothing the horses by feeding them carrots to distract them. That is all, except for one filly that had to be tranquilized.

Twelve hours later the van pulled into Sunshine Meadows. Despite being extremely tired, all weary occupants were eager to get off, despite sensing what would be a totally different environment than what they were accustomed to in Canada.

Horses are creatures of habit and normally follow a regular routine. Whenever that routine is disrupted or changed, some horses react and are hesitant to it.

The weather in Florida was warm—almost hot and humid. The palm trees looked completely different than the oaks, pines, and maples that were up north and the tropical birds were unlike the ones they had back home.

Looking out the trailer window, Junior observed numerous

horses as they trotted around an expansive dirt circle, pulling something he would later discover were called jog carts.

As the trailer pulled up in front of the barn several of the horses in the shed row bellowed out welcoming the newcomers.

Each yearling was allocated its own personal stall that would be his permanent winter home. After Junior checked out his new abode a young man entered proclaiming, "Hello, my name is Stefan and I will be taking care of you."

After carefully examining the colt, the Swedish groom told Chris, "*I really like this one. He reminds me of a colt I once took care of up north named Joie De Vie. He has a head like him and his conformation is similar.*"

"*Well I hope that's a good thing,*" laughed Chris.

"*A good thing is an understatement! Joie was the champion that year in New Jersey and Pennsylvania, and he won over $1 million in his career.*"

*****

Over the next few weeks the entire Christoforou Stable got broken to the jog cart; some did it easy and others were harder to break.

One of the fillies, a Sebastian K yearling that was purchased for $100,000, kicked the shaft of the cart, splintering it and cutting her leg in the process.

Another filly decided to buck while on the track, bracing her leg over the shaft, only to throw Chris out of the bike while she took off in frantic flight. Luckily, she was caught before she was seriously injured or hurt someone else.

Breaking Junior had been a piece of cake. In fact, he was TOO good. The only problem Chris had with the colt was he would fight the bit.

"**I'm not sure what that hard, cold thing is they keep putting in my mouth,**" Junior said to Sammy.

"**I heard them call it a 'bit'. Whatever it is, I hate it. It hurts!**"

By mid December most of the young trainees were jogging

three miles a day. Several of the more immature colts who were still in the playing mode would throw their heads or weave in and out around the grater that was there to keep the track relatively smooth.

One day while Junior was on the track jogging, a large egret flew too close, startling him. The colt jumped, bucked, and then switched into a high-speed trot. Caught completely off guard, Chris clutched the lines tight and steered the colt as straight as possible. When he returned to the stable two of the grooms were waiting there with their mouths agape.

Stefan grabbed the lines as he walked Junior back to the barn.

"Wow! Did you see that? He must have trotted a quarter in 33 seconds. And he never skipped a beat!" Stefan said.

"To be exact, I clocked him a quarter in 32 seconds!"

"I think we might just have something here, boss," said a proud Stefan as he patted Junior on the neck.

"After all, he is a Holiday Road from a Muscle Hill mare — and Holiday Road did win the Haughton Memorial the same day Muscle Hill won the Hambletonian!"

"Yes sir, this colt has some pedigree!"

*****

Unlike winter training in Canada under brutal conditions, the Florida trainees in Florida scantily missed days due to inclement weather. While South Florida is known for frequent, but intermittent showers, the strong sun and sandy texture quickly dries the track.

Like young children in kindergarten, the horses only missed days exercising when they got sick. And like youngsters who are apt at picking up bugs and viruses, should one yearling catch a cold it usually passed through the entire stable.

Junior's pal Sammy was one who never really bounced back after catching a bug, thus he fell behind the other colts so Chris decided to stop with him until they returned home in April.

But surprisingly Junior was keeping up with the top colts that had been approaching 2:20. Although he wasn't the "star pupil," he was considered one of the top five.

After the second month of breaking the colts and fillies, Chris called his father back home to give him the run down.

"Hey dad. Just calling to brief you on where we are now. So far my favorite is the Muscle Hill colt out of Dream On."

"Next, I like the Kadabra filly, No More Bras, out of Say No More; and last but not least I like Junior—the little orphan," Chris reported.

"Although, he is not so little anymore. In fact, he's one of my best looking colts."

"It's still early in the game, son. Let's not get too excited. We have a long way until we know who will rise to the top. Anything can happen, as you well know," said Mr. C.

"By the way—how is Junior's sister Elena doing?" Chris asked his dad.

"Ever since she was separated from her brother, Jack has had a problem with her. She's become a sulker and has gone off her feed."

"Not sure what to do just yet because she is such a nice filly and shows raw talent," Mr. C. replied.

*****

By the end of March the two-year-olds in the Christoforou stable were training in sets of three and four. The more advanced had approached the 2:18 level and Chris could not have been happier.

Junior had been elevated to set one for he was doing everything right and doing it easy. It was now the last week of training before they would be heading back to Canada. Once back home the young athletes would get a well deserved several weeks rest to help them re-acclimate to the colder conditions before resuming preparations for their stakes engagements.

On the last training day before shipping out, Chris was on the *Muscle Hill* colt, Stefan sat behind *Junior*, while a second trainer took the *Kadabra* filly, *No More Bras*.

As usual, Stefan kept Junior behind the others the first three quarters of a mile before tipping him out at the top of the stretch.

When he chirped, the colt swelled up and flew like a bat out of hell. With ears pinned back and head down, the colt trotted by the other two horses like they were standing still.

Heading back to the barn Stefan yelled to Chris, *"Holy moly, Chris. This is some kind of nice colt here."*

Chris nodded with pride.

"Shocked the hell out of me. Thought he was good, but not that good."

"He just keeps surprising me. I wonder where he will hit a wall?"

After giving Junior his obligatory bubble bath, Stefan proudly paraded him around the barn while feeding him his favorite peppermint candies he kept in his pocket.

"You're going to be my new champ, buddy. I bet you win the Maple Leaf Trot next year!"

"I wouldn't go that far, Stefan. Although he is pretty good, I've never had one win the Maple Leaf before!" Chris laughed.

"That's asking a little too much. Hell, I'll be thrilled if he's just a good Ontario Gold colt."

PHOTO GALLERY

Mama Emprize and her 2 kids- Junior and Elena

Introducing Emprize Hanover

Elena and Junior asleep in their bed

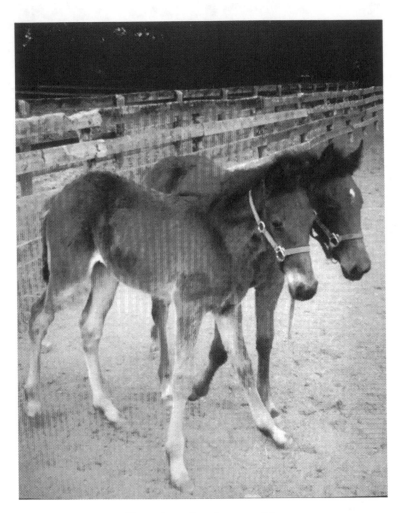

Enjoying the day outside

Kicking our heels up

Mama watching out while her babies enjoy lying in the sun

Mama grazing, while Junior rests

Time for dinner

Playing tag

Mama Emprize scratching her back

Trying to reach the green grass

Enjoying a little mother-daughter time

Elena following brother, Junior

Time for another drink

Elena getting brave, exploring on her own

Mama on guard while the kids graze

Junior is such a momma's boy

Elena and Junior going off on their own

What is this big thing? A new way to get a drink!

Mother and son time alone

Waiting to be fed

Mama resting while her kids are asleep

We even have to drink water together!

Just born. Emma feeding Junior his milk from a bottle

Best friends forever

7

Elena Trains in Canada

"The earth would be nothing without the people, but the man would be nothing without the horse."

First Line Training Center
Campellville, Ontario
January 2018

The winter of 2017 in Canada was unusually brutal. The temperatures remained well below normal and the snow accumulation had vastly exceeded the weatherman's most dire predictions.

At the Jack Moiseyev Stable, the two-year-olds in training had missed a considerable amount of days jogging due to the inclement weather. Several of the horses had been stopped and were turned out for the remainder of the year, for Jack didn't think they were ready to move forward just yet. Some were mentally immature; several sustained minor injuries while training, while ex-rays disclosed others had knees that were not fully closed.

Unlike some trainers who would continue training their babies even though their joints were not yet fully developed, Jack believed in stopping with them and let Mother Nature take it's course.

"If you have to start injecting acid into their joints before they even

race, chances are you will not have a racehorse that has longevity," Jack quoted.

And he was right for many two-year-olds that had been pushed and stressed, either end up with bow tendons, strained suspensorys or worse, a life altering career that ended way too soon.

Since the first day Elena was brought into the barn she had been a problem child. All day she would stand in the back of her stall sulking and intermittently go off her feed. She was definitely having a major separation anxiety attack being away from her mother and brother.

Although she was built like a colt---muscular and strong—she had lost a considerable amount of weight due to not eating. And Jack liked his young ones to have a little extra weight on at this stage for he knew that once they went into training, weight would quickly come off.

One day after Elena refused to go on the track, Jack was totally fed up and ready to throw the towel in.

"My patience is running out with this filly. I'm ready to send Elena to the next sale and let someone else put up with her antics," Jack scoffed.

"Just because a horse can run fast in the field doesn't mean it will be a racehorse," Jamie answered. *"Maybe Elena just doesn't want to race."*

She continued, *"And some horses aren't meant to be two-year-olds. Maybe you should stop with her and turn her out the rest of the year."*

"It's hard for me to do that for she definitely is by far one of the best-gaited trotters I have in the barn," Jack scoffed.

"But it seems to me that ever since she was taken from Junior, she has been heartbroken and lost her zest to live."

Luckily, the other freshman and sophomore horses in the Moiseyev barn were "good doer's" --they would eat no matter what you gave them. A horseman loves when they have a horse that is a good eater.

But if a horse gets off their food there are several things you can do. First, you try changing the feed hoping to find one that is pleasant to them. If that doesn't work you can "add" something like molasses, honey or even cut up fruit, like carrots and apples as an incentive. And the last resort is putting a goat or another small animal in the stall hoping this will entice them to eat before their new companion does.

Seeing that Jack tried everything else but getting a companion, this seemed like the obvious thing to do.

No matter what they did to try to make Elena happy, the bay filly would stand in the back of her stall with her head hung down. Her caretaker, Jamie, paid extra attention to her-- offering her treats, taking her out of the stall for long walks, and bought her so many toys her stall looked like an aisle at a TOYS R US store.

There were several Jolly Balls on the floor and one hanging up, but the obstinate filly ignored them all.

"*I really don't know what to do about Elena,*" Jack told Joanne one day.

"*Since the day she came in my barn she's been nothing but a problem. The sad thing is I believe she is one of the most talented fillies I have ever trained and has a ton of speed, but she just doesn't want to do it—at least not at this time.*"

"*You know Jack, Elena and Junior had an exceptional unique relationship. Being thrown together as they were is not your everyday situation. I believe she is heartbroken and mourning for her brother,*" Joanne said.

"*Well then we have a real problem because they will not be together again and she has to get over it!*" Jack scoffed.

"*Maybe you should try getting her a little friend. You know a goat or a pony: something to put in her stall to keep her company. It's worth a try.*"

"*You might have a point Joanne. Jamie and I were just discussing that the other day. I'll go to the auction and get her a pony tomorrow,*" Jack said. "*It's certainly worth a try. For her sake it better help.*"

*****

Early the next morning Jack and Emma drove to the local horse auction where they purchased a five-year-old pony named

Dressy Bessy. Bessy was a roan Shetland who had been consigned to the sale due to her owners' sudden death. She was a sweet, quiet filly that stood 10 hands tall.

When they returned to the barn Elena was grazing in her paddock. Jack took the pony off the trailer and walked her over to the paddock Elena was in.

As Bessy cautiously approached the mare, Elena let out a loud squeal and trotted away, but within a few minutes the odd couple was side-by-side eating grass off the ground.

When they were brought in the barn several hours later Elena allowed her new little friend to lie in the corner, making sure she had enough room.

At feed time the two shared a large feed bucket that was placed on the ground. Elena preferred to eat out of the same bucket as her new friend, just as she had once done with her brother, Junior. In no time, the filly was eating like a champ and had put on a hundred pounds.

The next couple weeks Jack left Elena out in the paddock with Bessy all day and kept her off the track, trying to sweeten her up a bit.

One day while watching the odd couple grazing in the paddock Jack told Joanne, *"I'm so glad that Elena has accepted her new friend."*

"But the party's over. Her mini vacation is over. Tomorrow I'm starting her back jogging. I'm anxious to see if her attitude is any better on the track. For her sake it better be, or else she may have to find a new home."

"Give her a chance, Jack. This little girl has been through a lot in her short life," said Joanne.

*****

Purchasing a companion for a horse is nothing new. Throughout the years there have been many horses that needed a friend to be by their side.

The ornery Thoroughbred champion *Smarty Jones* had a pony named *Butterscotch*. The 1990 Kentucky Derby winner, *Unbridled,* had a pony named *Mustard,* and the great *Seabiscuit* relied on several four-legged companions: a horse named *Pumpkin,* a dog named *Pocatell,* and a spider monkey named *Jo-Jo.*

Then of course the folks at Roosevelt Raceway on Long Island prevented what could have evolved into an international incident by obtaining the perfect goat companion for the French champion Kracovie who had been shipped there to contest the Roosevelt International Race. It appeared someone had forgotten to load the goat with Kracovie on the plane ride over and the champion mare was beside herself with grief, until an adequate companion was located.

Some horses are more needy than others and some just have that maternal instinct and need and want someone to mother and dote on.

As stated earlier, horses are not loners by nature and are naturally suited to life with at least one companion, so when a racehorse becomes sour from living alone in a stall and refuses to eat and begins to sulk, experienced trainers immediately obtain a pony, goat, dog, or even a chicken to placate the agitated horse.

Also, when valuable horses are too spirited or accident prone and cannot be turned out with another horse, ponies and miniature horses can make great companions in keeping them company.

The following day when Jack took Elena on the track for her daily exercise little Bessy stood by the fence in observation. It was as if Elena was showing off for her little playmate for she would proudly trot by with her tail cocked and head held high. Little Bessy stood there, eyes fixated on her adopted mother and wouldn't relax until they were both back in the stall together.

One extremely breezy day, a tree branch snapped off making a loud crackling sound, spooking Bessy while she was tied to the fence watching Elena. The pony broke loose with her lead shank still snapped on and commenced running down the racetrack. When Elena spotted the pony running loose she pinned her ears back, put her head down, and took off in hot pursuit.

By the time Jack and Elena caught up with Bessy, Jamie had

retrieved her. As Jack looked at his stopwatch it revealed the mare trotted a quarter in 29 seconds!

"Wow! Unbelievable, I knew this girl had it in her," he told Jamie back at the barn. *"But I didn't think she was that quick and smooth."*

"You know Jamie, I keep forgetting she is by E.L. Titan, and he was no slouch. He almost beat Father Patrick in the Breeders Crown at the Meadowlands, so Elena definitely has the credentials to be a good one."

"She looked awesome, Jack, but I hope this doesn't mean we will have to tote Bessy along with her every time she races," she laughed.

"Hey, whatever it takes we will do. I now have a very good feeling about this little girl," he said as he patted Elena on the head.

8

A Brief Reunion

"If you want to know about a horse's life, just look into his eyes."

April 2018
First Line Training Center
Moffat, Ontario

It was the third week in April when Chris and his stable of two-year-olds headed back to Canada. It had been an eventful and exciting winter, to say the least.

Chris had been very happy with his young equine students and thought he just might have one or two serious stake prospects in the group. He liked the *Muscle Hill* colt named *Mr. Muscle Man*, and he was high on the orphan Junior, who was officially now named *Fleetwood*.

These two colts seemed to be ahead of the rest, as they had both trained in 2:05. And they did it easy!

Junior was a pleasure to have in the barn and the perfect colt. He took care of himself—lying down several times a day to rest. Most horsemen believe that a good horse takes care of himself—and that is exactly what Junior did. When he was turned out in the paddock, he behaved like a perfect gentleman—unlike his stable mate, *Mr. Muscle Man* whose hormones were now raging.

Stefan grew extremely attached to Junior and vice versa.

When Junior's buddy Sammy shipped home after hurting his tendon back in February, Junior seemed to gravitate towards his caretaker instead of another horse.

The two would take long daily walks and were quite a sight for sore eyes. Stefan was a good-looking blond hair, blue-eyed, Swedish man and Junior was one of the handsomest colts on the track.

The female grooms were enamored with the young Swede, but he wasn't interested in settling down with any girl just yet. After all, he was only twenty-nine years old and knew that having a girlfriend would take time away from Junior and he wasn't about to let that happen for he was 100% dedicated to his colt.

He remembered when he was in New Jersey several years earlier taking care of Joie De Vie. His girlfriend, a nineteen-year-old named Heidi became extremely jealous of his relationship with his horse. Stefan thought her attitude was ridiculous and childish and hated when she would pout because he wanted to spend extra time with the colt, instead of her.

One day Heidi gave him an ultimatum: it was her or Joie. Guess who won? Yep, Stefan kicked Heidi to the curb and Joie De Vie was voted "Horse of the Year" the end of the year.

Stefan told his buddies that women would have to be put on the back burner—at least one more year—for his new colt, *Fleetwood*, was just as talented as Joie was.

And it's not every day that you get to take care of a racehorse like Junior. In fact, some people never get that experience.

During their evening walks, Stefan would sit in the grass holding the lead while his colt calmly grazed, rooting the ground for bits of clover. When Stefan arrived in the barn early in the morning, Junior would greet him with a loud whinny and shake his head.

Of course Stefan was prejudiced and spoiled his four-legged friend. Ever since that day in Florida when the young man first laid eyes on the colt, Stefan knew he was something special, so it was no surprise when it was time for him to return home to Sweden in April, he decided to go to Canada with Chris.

And that was exactly what Chris was hoping for. He knew from personal experience that when a groom and his horse connect like these two had it is beneficial for everyone if they remain together.

There have been times in a racehorse's life when a horse grows extremely close to his caretaker. Grooms, or caretakers are very important to their horse and are not given the respect, recognition and praise they deserve.

The groom is directly responsible for the daily care of the horse and plays a very important role and therefore a major contributor to the success of a racehorse. In fact, some people say that the groom is the most important person in a racehorse's life—even more so than the trainer.

I, myself, agree.

A perfect example was the great Thoroughbred *Man o' War,* and his caretaker and best friend, Will Harbut. After Harbut died suddenly it is said that Man o' War was so crestfallen he pined away and died less than a month later of a broken heart.

It is a known fact that people have passed away shortly after someone they have been with for years' dies. And there have also been reported cases of a dog who has pined himself to death after losing his master. So, why not a horse?

And we can't forget the true story of Eddie "Shorty" Sweat and his legendary horse the immortal *Secretariat.* Shorty loved "Big Red," as he affectionately called the horse, and the two became inseparable.

It is said that Eddie "listened" to Secretariat with his heart and with his ears and that the horse responded.

Sweat was known for his saying, "Show 'em (the horse) that you're trying to help 'em. Love 'em. Talk to 'em."

Perhaps Eddie Sweat was the first "horse whisperer?"

Stefan and Junior had that same type of relationship. There was no need for words as Junior knew exactly what his caretaker wanted before he was even asked. When it was time to graze in the grass, the colt would stretch his neck over the stall gate and grab the lead with his mouth. And whenever it was time for his daily bath the horse seemed to help Stefan do his job. He would drop his head for his groom to suds up his foretop and raise his tail to make sure he got all the dirt between his rear legs.

Back at the Moiseyev Stable, Jack and his students had survived a brutally cold and snowy winter. Unfortunately there had been many "snow days," as the track would be too icy and slick for the horses to jog.

The "star" pupil was a colt named *Roscoe* who Jackie Mo was high on.

He also really liked the filly Elena, whose registered name was *Peristera,* although she could be quite a handful at times. But ever since Jack purchased Bessy for Elena, she was a different horse.

She started eating and in fact would eat as much as Jamie would offer her. She never stood in the back of the stall sulking anymore and was one of the most pleasant horses to be around in the stable.

Of course the mare refused to go anywhere without her shadow. Elena truly thought the 10 hands pony was her biological child for she watched over her like a protective mother would.

And Bessy was just as attached to the mare. The pony would fret when she didn't see Elena, so the pint-sized horse went everywhere with her: when she exercised, bathed or grazed. They were inseparable—24 hours a day, 7 days a week.

*****

The spring of 2018 Chris decided to relocate and train at First Line Training Center, unlike the previous years when he stabled at Classy Lane Training Center. After the devastating fire that took place at Classy Lane a few years earlier, Chris could not bear to go back there.

In that horrific accident dozens of innocent horses succumbed to the fire, leaving behind many broken hearts. (Having had one of my own horses die in that fire I can say it's something nobody should ever have to go through.)

At First Line, Chris was stabled several barns away from Jack

Moiseyev. Being there were hundreds of horses stabled there and only so many turn out paddocks available, each stable was designated two.

Whenever the equine athletes were done exercising and bathed they enjoyed some playtime in the assigned field located behind the barns for an hour or two.

One particular day when Elena and Bessy were enjoying the crisp, cool weather in the paddock, Stefan walked Junior to the blacksmith, having to pass by the mare and pony.

As Junior walked by he began bucking and rearing. Because this was totally unlike his colt, it caught Stefan off guard and Junior broke loose. The colt trotted over to the pen where Elena and Bessy were grazing, ran up to the fence and stood there nose to nose with Elena.

At first, little Bessy feeling threatened by the new stranger became frantic and began running, bucking and bellowing. The chaos spread like wildfire and soon every horse turned out in the adjoining paddocks began acting up.

The trainers and grooms scurried to their horses to calm them down, making sure they didn't harm themselves. When Jack and Jamie arrived at Elena's paddock they were shocked to see Elena and Junior nuzzling one another; necks intertwined.

Bessy, unsure of what was happening to her mother, cowered under Elena, rubbing her little body against the mare.

Junior, not sure what to think of this strange little creature began sniffing her. Frightened, the pony let out a blood-curdling sound, but Elena quickly assured her all was well.

"Do you think Junior knows this is Elena?" Jamie questioned Jack.

"It certainly appears that way. It's been six months since they saw one another but I bet they hadn't forgotten who they were."

As Stefan hooked Junior to the lead shank and walked him away, Elena let out a whinny and Junior called back.

"And people think horses are dumb! They're smarter than most people I know, and have feelings, too. I believe these two

horses have a special bond that will never be broken," Stefan told Jamie.

*****

After the incident in the paddock, Junior and Elena did not see each other again, but didn't forget one another. At times Elena would whinny while she was jogging on the track and from a distant, Junior would answer.

Over the next few months the Jack Moiseyev and Chris Christoforou Stables prepared for the upcoming stake races that would soon be taking place.

The first baby races would be held at Mohawk Racetrack on June 7. Although Junior had trained down nicely, he was still considered second best to *Mr. Muscle Man.* That was, until one day when the *Muscle Hill* colt got his leg caught in the fence in the paddock and tore his tendon.

Chris was deeply disappointed for he knew the colt would not be ready for his first stake—and perhaps miss the entire year. Fortunately, he still had his little 'orphan,' Junior.

"Well buddy, it looks like all the pressure is on you now," Chris told the colt.

"Don't you worry about this boy. I told you from the very first time I saw him he's gonna be a champ," Stefan laughed.

*****

Meanwhile at the Moiseyev Stable, Jack had several serious potential stake candidates. There was a two-year-old pacing colt named *Roscoe* who was a big, good-looking pacer and there was Elena—the trotting filly by *Emprize Hanover.*

Ever since Jack bought Elena the pony, the two-year-old mare had become a dream horse. She seemed to love nurturing and mothering her little one. After a training session, Elena would lie down in the thick bed of straw with Bessy close by.

And when anyone would come to visit and offer carrots to

Elena, she would nudge the pony in front of her; making sure they acknowledged her friend, too.

By the middle of May, Elena had trained down to 2:02--- an exceptional mile and the fastest time of any two-year-old at the training center that year.

"I think this little girl is ready to rock and roll," Jack confided to Jamie.

"She sure is the best filly I have ever taken care of. I have high hopes for my princess," replied Jamie.

9

And They're Off

"Motherhood: All love begins and ends there."
Robert Browning

June 2018
Mohawk Raceway
Toronto, Canada

After several months of training and a few unexpected heartaches that arose along the way, the time had finally arrived. The two-year-old pacers and trotters that had been in training for the past seven months and had survived the rigorous schedule were ready to make their debut in the baby races at Mohawk Racetrack.

Out of the ten yearlings that Chris Christoforou originally shipped to South Florida in November, three were ready to show their stuff and considering the percentage of horses that actually make it to the races, Chris was quite pleased with the odds.

Thirty per cent is not as good as he hoped for, but considering that several horses got sick and never quite bounced back, and a few others sustained injuries and had to be stopped, Chris was content with the three that were ready to go.

Overall, of the approximately 80 foals that were shipped to Sunshine Meadows that winter, approximately 50-60% would successfully navigate the course and make the races as a freshman.

And whether they would actually make an appearance to the winners' circle—well, that was another matter all together.

Chris had been training a pacing colt by *Sportsmaster* named *Mr. Athlete* that he thought was exceptional. The colt had been good all winter until the last month when he decided he didn't want to be a racehorse, and since he was a stud they decided to castrate him and turn him out until the next year.

That is not uncommon, for there are many two-year-olds that look promising while training and do everything right and then one day they literally "hit a brick wall." Maybe they will train down to 2:10 before they let you know "that's all they are gonna go at that time," and others may train down to 2:05 when they call it a day.

But for trainers the real heartbreaker is when you have a horse train down to 2:00 or faster and you think you have a world-beater, and then they refuse to go any faster.

Chris had also been high all winter long on the beautiful trotting filly sired *by Kadabra* out of *Say No More* named *No More Bras*. And last but not least was the orphan colt, Junior, aka/*Fleetwood*. These two young equine athletes were ready to proceed.

So it was up to *Junior aka/Fleetwood* and *No More Bras* to carry the stable.

*****

Baby races are *almost* as exciting as stake races for it is the unknown of which filly or colt would rise to the top. The funny thing is that many times the one horse that trainers think will be "the one," usually aren't. And then there is the average student that showed his trainer he had potential, but just hadn't put it all together yet that suddenly blossoms.

The first set of baby races were held at Mohawk on Friday June 7.

The morning of the race it began to rain and continued coming down until right before race one was called to post.

Several cautious trainers scratched their horses as they watched the ground grow slippery and develop dangerous ruts.

There was a total of six races set to go that day: three for two-year-old trotters and three for two-year-old pacers. In a baby race there is no purse money allotted-- but that didn't matter to the horsemen, for the colts and fillies in the Canadian sire stakes would be going for over a million dollars in purses that season.

Junior/Fleetwood drew post position four in the first race. All week long Stefan was a bundle of nerves.

"I think you're more nervous than I am," said Chris. *"It's just a baby race. The one that counts is next week."*

"I know. But this is "MY" baby. Junior means the world to me and I have believed in him since the first day I walked into his stall."

Since the baby races are held at Mohawk during the morning hours, it wouldn't be a problem for the freshman athletes to "race under the lights" like they do at night. For some horses racing under the lights is never a problem, but for others they see shadows and try to jump them—thus causing them to go off stride. This is why many horses wear shadow rolls or blinkers. This equipment partially restricts the horse's vision and helps him concentrate on what is in front of him, rather than objects on the ground.

Being the perfect gentleman that he had been since the day he was born, Junior behaved like a pro, walking into the paddock as if he were walking into his stall to retire for the night.

Chris had taken his babies behind the starting gate at Sunshine Meadows and schooled them each several times as he believed in educating them behind the starting gate early.

As the starter called the horses to the gate, Chris guided Fleetwood into the assigned fourth position.

Going to the gate several of the green, young trotters broke stride as the car sped up, while Junior eased out and fell in third. The leader reached the quarter pole in a speedy 27 seconds— much faster than Junior had ever trained in.

After getting to the half in 57 seconds, the leader tired and made a nasty break as his driver eased him to the outside –steering him out of the way from the trailing horses.

With the frontrunner off stride, Junior moved up to second place, as the timer flashed 1:26.4 at the ¾ pole. Chris really didn't expect his colt to keep up as this was by far the fastest Junior had ever been in.

But the colt that had a rough start at birth and defied the odds, took himself out of the hole and blew by the leader while his stunned driver sat there steering him.

As they crossed the finish line Chris looked at the timer and was shocked to see it read 1:56.2!!! And this was over a track rated "good!"

By the time Chris returned to the paddock Stefan was waiting there flashing a bright smile that would have lit up any dark day. Jumping up and down like a cheerleader whose boyfriend had just scored a winning touchdown, Stefan yelled, *"I told you Chris! This boy of ours is a mighty good one!"*

"I always knew he had the speed but didn't expect to see it this early in the game," the proud driver commented.

"I have to admit I didn't have as much confidence in him as you did and I certainly didn't want to go that fast in his first race, but I didn't ask him at all."

"This little bugger didn't want to sit in the hole and at the ¾ pole he pinned his ears back, put his head down, and dug in like an old pro!"

"I just hope it didn't take too much out of him, for next week we will be going for some serious money and he will have to race against much tougher competition."

As Stefan proudly led his colt into the paddock to strip off the equipment and bathe him, several grooms ran over to congratulate him.

Oblivious to what he had just accomplished, Junior burrowed his sweaty nose into Stefan's pocket searching for his reward—his peppermint candy. He knew his friend always had a pocket full of peppermints hidden for him as a treat.

"I hate to brag, but didn't I tell you I had the best two-year-old colt this year?" Stefan said to his friend.

As he was enjoying a well-deserved bubble bath, the colt from another mother thought, *"What is all this commotion about? They didn't know I was a good one? Just because my mom died at birth and I beat the odds to get to the races—they haven't seen anything yet!"*

"I'm the underdog who is going to make a name. The Rocky Balboa of the standardbred world."

"The only thing is I hope my sister, Elena, and mother hear about this and are proud of me."

*****

Unbeknownst to the colt that was now the talk of the racetrack, his sister Elena, now officially called *Peristera,* was also in to race that day. She was in race five, drawing the seven hole, along with seven other two-year-old fillies.

Jackie Mo had trained her down to 2:02 several weeks earlier and was quite pleased with her and was hoping to go a mile in 2:00 that day. Ever since they bought Elena the pony Bessy, the filly was content with her little companion and as long as she was toted along with her, Elena cooperated fully.

Of course it was cumbersome toting the pony everywhere Elena went, but it was worth it to Jack.

As I said earlier there have been many racehorses that have had companions, but their little friends usually were not hauled everywhere they went—especially to the races. But Jack discovered the hard way that it would not be that way with his horse.

One day when he shipped Elena to Mohawk to train, he was in a hurry and completely forgot to bring along Bessy. By the time he realized it they were halfway to the racetrack and he didn't have time to go back.

Once Elena was unloaded and in the paddock, the mare sulked, pinned her ears back and refused to go. From that day on, little Bessy went everywhere with Elena.

*****

On the day of the baby races, as Jamie walked Elena out of the paddock to warm up before the race, little Bessy went berserk. Whether it was because it was a strange new environment or all the horses were parading in and out-- the pony bellowed and kicked the stall, upsetting all the other horses. The paddock judge summoned Jack into his office and warned him that if he didn't calm the pony down, she would have to leave.

"What are we going to do, Jamie?" Jack inquired. *"You know Elena will refuse to do anything if she doesn't have her friend with her.*

"When you go out to race with Elena I will walk Bessy up to the fence so she can see her," Jamie said.

Once the two horses could see one another, the pony calmed down and Elena paraded out to compete in her very first race.

Elena was coming out of the seventh position, which is on the far outside, but Jack thought that it might be a good thing for Bessy could see her clearly and vice versa.

Once he got Elena settled behind the gate, she became racy and got on the bit. As the starting car doors swung open, Elena flung her head once and then proudly held it in the air, ears pointed forward. She zoomed to the front, trotting a very fast 28 seconds.

"Whoa, girl. Where the hell are you running off to? There's no fire," a worried Jack yelled to his filly.

But Elena continued grabbing on and opened up, reaching the half in a very speedy 57 seconds. Just as Jack got the filly settled down, another freshman trotted up to her sending Elena to the ¾'s in 1:26. When the filly got alongside Elena, she pinned her ears back and took off, putting the other horse away.

As he crossed the wire, Jack gazed at the timer. He thought he read it wrong as he saw the time 1:56.1! When they returned to the paddock, everyone was applauding.

"Jeez, Jack. Why did you go so much with her? You know she's only been in 2:02!" Jamie asked. *"And it's a muddy track!"*

"I didn't make her go that fast—I couldn't hold her. And when that other filly got up beside her, she took off. I just hope she didn't hurt herself," he said defensively.

After Elena was stripped of her muddy equipment, she enjoyed her bath while her little friend, Bessy stood right beside her. Once loaded in the van to go back home, the pony lied down in the trailer next to Elena's legs.

"You really scared me. What the heck were you doing out there, Elena?" Bessy asked.

"I was racing. I wanted to make everyone proud of me. But I had no idea I had to go that fast. My legs are a bit achy so I can't wait to go back to our stall and rest."

As Bessy dozed off Elena thought, *"I sure wish mama and Junior were here to see me. I beat all the other horses so I guess that means I did good?"*

10

An Unexpected Setback

"A Horse doesn't care how much you may know—until he knows how much you care."

Summer/Fall 2018
Toronto, Canada

After the two-year-old baby races, *Peristera* and *Fleetwood* (still known by many as Elena and Junior) were once again the talk of Ontario. The pair of horses that made the front page of every newspaper in Canada with their remarkable story two years earlier had impressed horsemen with their winning efforts.

The first Canadian Gold Sire Stakes was scheduled to race on Saturday, June 22. Chris was pleased with how his new superstar Junior came out of the baby race. It was if he hadn't raced at all for the colt was jumping and playing in the paddock like a frisky yearling. He was perfectly sound and his legs were nice and tight.

Every day Stefan would take his pride and joy on several walks in a meadow close by the barn where Junior would eat the green grass. Stefan was extremely proud of the colt, as was Chris.

"You have done a great job with Junior, Stefan. You really love him and he knows it. That is why he is so happy and racing well."

"Thanks, boss, but you have to keep these guys happy if you want them to race good. That's the secret. They aren't machines, they are living creatures that have feelings and emotions."

"They can't talk and tell us where they hurt. I know one thing, when I'm hurting I don't want to run." Stefan said.

*****

The day after the baby race Chris had his veterinarian go over Junior from head to toe with a fined toothed comb, making sure everything was good to go. After the colt was examined the vet told Chris, "You have a real nice colt here. He doesn't have a pimple on him, and he's the most well behaved stud I've seen in a long time."

In the first leg of the Gold, Junior drew the sixth position in a field of nine. The purse was a hefty $180,000. There were three divisions of colts that would compete for the monies; thus each division would go for $60,000.

But when you least expect the unexpected to happen, it does. Murphy's Law says that if anything can go wrong, it will, and it did in the Christoforou barn the night before the baby race.

On the morning of the race there was unexpected chaos in the barn. It appeared that one of the horses—a three-year-old filly-- escaped from her stall the night before and decided to throw a party. When Stefan arrived at 5 o'clock in the morning to feed, the barn was in shambles.

Feed cans were overturned and harness bags were scattered across the floor. One young stallion tried to join the filly but was unable to break out of his stall and in the process scraped his leg rather noticeably.

The jog cart that was to go to the paddock with Junior had a broken shaft and the tires on the race bike were flat.

After the barn was cleaned up and the horses settled down, Stefan shipped Junior to Mohawk Raceway where Chris would later meet them.

As he did in the baby race, while the horses lined up behind the gate, Junior had his nose pressed right on it. But unlike the previous race where he sat patiently in a hole, when the gate opened the colt was on top by two lengths. Easily in hand, all Chris had to do was steer his little trotting machine to the wire.

He reached the finish line three lengths ahead of the second horse in a time of 1:56.1.

That was 1/5 second faster than he went the previous time!

Sitting straight up on the bike like a proud peacock with ruffled feathers, Chris guided his colt into the winner circle where Stefan was anxiously waiting. Along with the groom was a crowd of people there to congratulate him, including Chris Sr., Joanne, and Emma.

Ken Middleton, the track announcer shouted over the loud speaker, "*Coming back to the winners circle is Fleetwood, the unofficial winner of the third race.*"

"*The two-year-old colt by Holiday Road out of the mare Noble Flirt just set a track record for two-year-old trotting colts in an impressive 1:56.1.*"

He continued, "*This is the colt that many call Junior: a brother from another mother, and all you locals know how this story goes. I guess this proves that anything is possible in horse racing.*"

When Junior was done with his bath and had cooled out, Stefan made a fluffy stall of golden yellow straw for the colt to rest in. It was so thick that when the horse walked in, the straw covered his knees.

The proud Swede opened a bag of carrots and fed the obliging horse several. On race nights Stefan liked to feed his horses a warm bran mash. Since this was the first time Junior had ever been fed bran mash, he didn't quite know what to think of the sweet, sticky substance. He buried his mouth in it and swished the food around, getting more up his nose than in his mouth.

As the content colt removed his head from the feed tub, he curled his lip, flashing teeth covered with molasses. Laughing, Emma snapped a picture.

"*Guess he likes it, eh?*" Chris laughed.

*****

This was also the day to be Elena's debut, but an unfortunate situation occurred the day after her baby race that would alter the plans for the filly and her owners.

The morning after the race, Jamie noticed the filly's tendon blew up. Jack immediately called the vet to take ex-rays. After the film was developed, the vet grudgingly informed Jackie Mo that she had a slight tear in her high suspensory on the right front leg.

"Oh great, doc. This is by far the best filly in the barn. I had some big plans for her," said a disgruntled Jack.

"I'm sorry Jack. I wish I had better news for you, but that monster mile she put in did a job on her suspensory. It could be worse. It's not that bad, but it's bad enough that if she were my horse, I wouldn't race her."

"We can try injecting it or freeze it but I'm not sure how she will race. It is a mild tear and I have seen many horses race with this type of injury and do okay. But being this is a young filly with potential, I'm not sure I would do that."

When the vet left, Jack grudgingly called Mr. C. and told him the bad news.

"Oh damn it. Just when I have a good filly this happens. That's my luck!"

Mr. C. cried.

"I know, Chris. I'm as sick as you, for I know she is a good one. We will do what we can and see what happens," Jack said.

For the next several weeks Jamie religiously attended to Elena's leg; icing it, wrapping it with cold bandages, and poulticed it at night. The swelling came down a little but whenever Jack would test her, the filly would favor the leg and get on a line.

*****

Three days before the race Jack grudgingly called the filly's owner to tell him the bad news.

"I'm afraid we have to quit with Elena this year," Jackie told Mr. C. on the phone.

"I know you are just as disappointed as I am, but I truly believe this is one special filly and if we go on with her she will be nothing."

Although Chris Sr. was deeply disappointed, he knew that if they tried to race Elena, it would hurt her in the long run. This was not his first rodeo for he had been through this a time or two before and knew that racing Elena would only be harmful. So

Jack and Mr. C. decided to call it a year and hung up her harness for the rest of the 2018 season.

As for her brother, Junior. That year he raced a total of eight races in the Gold, winning five and breaking several track records, amassing a whopping $800,000.

Not bad for an orphan, eh?

11

Making the Big Time

"I am a great champion: when I ran the ground shook and the sky opened up and mere mortals parted the way to victory, and I met my owner in the winners circle where he put a blanket of flowers on my back."

Spring 2019
Mohawk Racetrack
Ontario, Canada

At the end of the 2018 racing season, Chris Christoforou Jr. opted to stay in Canada for the winter to train. Although he had enjoyed sunny Florida the year before, breaking his colts and fillies, Chris's dad wanted to watch his new crop of yearlings be broke.

That's one of the things most horse owners enjoy--- watching their four-legged babies train and develop into athletes.

They had big plans for their new superstar *Fleetwood* and staked him to the Gold Sires Stakes and several other high profile races in Canada.

One day while dad and son was sitting in the office at the barn going over the stake schedule, Chris Sr. asked his son, *"Hey, what would you think if I stake Junior to the Maple Gold Leaf Trot that takes place in September? I know it's a long shot, having to race against older boys, but it's worth a shot."*

"I don't know dad. I think that's asking a lot from Junior. I'd hate

to see you spend that kind of money on a shot in the dark," Chris Jr. answered.

But after Chris saw the dismal look on his dad's face he said, "If you really want to give it a try, we will. It's your money."

"Hell. I spend more money on things that aren't half as important as this. If he has any shot, I want to go for it," Mr. C. stammered.

"After all, it's not every day you get a colt with this kind of talent and speed. I've been in the business for decades and although I've had some good ones, I never had one good enough to run in the Maple Leaf."

*****

Deep down inside Chris thought there could be a slim chance that his colt could possibly pick up a check--if he got a good trip and things went his way-- but he never thought he could win a race like the Maple Leaf Trot. That was asking a lot, especially from a mere three-year-old.

Just getting a check seemed like a long shot and the one thing he was sure of is that he didn't want to take the heart and spirit out of his colt. Junior had done everything right since day one and gave 100% in every race. He was a very game horse.

Chris had experienced in the past when racing a horse over his head or putting him in against much tougher horses, it takes the heart out of the horse and can permanently ruin him.

But on the other hand, he didn't want to go against his dad. Chris Sr. had been in the business for 50 years and this colt was his baby and dream. So after it was decided that the colt would be entered in the big race, Chris gave Junior a well earned three-weeks off. During the day he would turn him out in the paddock --weather permitting.

The colt enjoyed the mini vacation, as he would trot from one end of the paddock to another, nibbling on whatever grass was left and enjoyed the remaining cool days of fall.

During the time off, Junior seemed to mature. Although his legs were completely clean, his neck seemed to be longer and there was something compelling about his head.

His shoulders were stronger this year with the right amount

of slope, and his withers—the bone at the base of his neck ran smoothly down his back. But what Chris noticed most were the colt's hips. They appeared more angular and jutted upward---making his long lean legs stick out more.

As he had always done since he was a yearling, Junior took good care of himself by lying down in his stall. But when he was turned out in the paddock after his daily exercise, the colt seemed to be more alert and alive than he had been the year before. Perhaps he was getting confident and a bit cocky after winning his races?

One habit the colt had was ever since he was a young colt he loved to roll in his stall after a bath. Stefan loved seeing him do that for he believed when a horse rolls, he can't be hurting anywhere.

But one day when Junior was rolling he got too close to the side of the stall and got cast. Chris was on the track jogging another horse and Stefan was busy getting fresh drinking water for Junior when he heard the loudest banging.

Knowing too well what the horrific sound meant, Stefan dropped his pail and ran to Junior's stall. When he arrived he found the colt with his rear legs crossed over each other; the bottom one wedged into the side wood panel.

Freaking out, but trying not to alarm the nervous colt anymore than he already was, the Swede slowly walked into the stall. By then Chris arrived back at the barn and ran to assist Stefan.

As the groom sat softly on Junior's head, talking to him in a quiet calming tone, Chris grabbed the colts' tail and yanked on it, flipping his legs apart.

Once the colt was free, he stood up and shook.

"*Jeez, Junior. You scared the living daylights out of me. Don't you EVER do that again,*" Stefan pleaded as sweat dropped from his brow.

"*You don't have to worry about that, Stefan. This boy is getting a double stall TODAY!*"

"*Take Money Bags out of the next stall and put him down the row in stall 14.*"

"I'm calling maintenance to come here and take these boards out now."
"We can't take a chance of anything like this ever happening again,"
Chris said.

*****

Although Junior wasn't castrated and remained intact, he had always been a perfect stallion. But this year the colt seemed to "come alive" a bit. Whenever a mare would come in season and Junior got a good whiff, he let everyone know, "Yes, he was still a stud indeed." For that reason, Chris cautiously kept all the mares on the backside of the barn.

*****

Stefan and Junior remained inseparable. In fact there were even several nights when the Swedish groom would fall asleep on the couch in the tack room and spend the entire evening at the barn.

When Chris arrived at the barn in the early hours of the morning, he would find Stefan either sleeping in a chair in front of Junior's stall or in with the colt, grooming him.

"Don't you think you should go home at night, buddy? I mean it got down to 10 degrees last night. I don't need you to get pneumonia."

"I'm fine, Chris. Thanks for being concerned, but I'm right where I want to be and Junior wants me here, too."

"I have to watch our star, for anything can happen. He can get cast again, a horse can get loose---ANYTHING!" "No, I need to stay here."

*****

Several barns over at the Moiseyev Stable, Elena's leg had healed nicely to where it was hard to see that she had injured it the year before. Her caretaker, Jamie, took exceptional care of the three-year-old filly and everyone said she was the reason Elena's leg had healed so well.

Every day the young woman would sit down on a pillow on the cold cement floor and rub the injured leg for half an hour at a time-- massaging it--- circulating the blood to help the healing process along. And of course Bessy the pony would be lying close by making sure nothing happened to her mom.

"*I can't believe how good Elena's leg looks Jamie. I owe it all to you,*" Jack stated.

"*Thanks, but lets wait until she trains down to see if it holds up,*" she said.

*****

There were times, especially at night, when everybody went home and the barn was quiet that Elena would think about her brother, Junior.

"**I sure hope you're okay, Junior. It's been a long time since I saw you that day in the paddock.**"

"**Bessy is wonderful and I love her, but she can't take your place. Nobody will ever take your place.**"

*****

Chris began training his horses in sets. Sometimes there were four horses in a set and other times there would be as many as eight. But no matter how many horses or how old they were --Junior would win most of the time. The little colt was the raciest and gamest horse Chris ever sat behind.

It didn't matter if Junior cut the mile or came from behind. As soon as he hit the top of the lane the colt would find another gear. He pinned his ears back and moved his head in unison swaying from side to side as he dug in.

At times it appeared that Junior taunted the other horses as he followed behind, lollygagging. To those observing it looked like the horses in front had slowed down at the top of the stretch, waiting on the young colt.

First, Junior's nose would slowly appear to be edging up to the horse in front, next came his head, and then his shoulders. By the time the set of horses crossed the finish line, Junior was lengths ahead of the others, with still some gas left in his motor.

Chris trained Junior in 1:58 before the first race of the season was to take place. He thought that his colt was tight enough for he had accumulated a lot of training miles over the winter.

Luckily, the winter of 2018-2019 was rather mild in Toronto. The horses didn't miss many days jogging, thus they were not behind the horses that were training in Florida the winter months.

Every year in Canada there were the same big name stables to watch out for: Casie Coleman, Tony Alagna, Richard Moreau, Jimmy Takter, Bob McIntosh and the newest young trainer, Travis Cullen.

Racing in Canada is one of the best racing circuits and many top horses call the province home. *Shambala, Bee In Charge, Caprice Hill, Marion Marauder, Resolve, L.A. Delight* and the champion *Swan for All* mare, *Hannelore Hanover*, are just some of the monster racehorses that have raced in Canada.

And each year there's always a new stable that comes out of the woodwork introducing a new superstar.

Perhaps this will be the year for Chris Christoforou to win his first Maple Leaf Trot with *Fleetwood*—or maybe Jackie Mo's *Peristera* aka/ Elena could be the next filly to beat the big boys?

Only the racing God's know for sure!

*****

The first leg of the three-year-old trotting colts was set to go on Saturday, July 6, and the three-year-old fillies would race the night before on Friday, July 5.

Elena drew post two and was second favorite in a field of ten. She qualified two weeks earlier and won the race by an impressive five lengths in a time of 1:58. That was exactly how fast Jack wanted the mare to trot and was extremely happy she came out of the race sound.

In the paddock Elena behaved like a perfect lady since her companion, Bessy was right alongside of her. Jack had to get an approval by the officials and judges that the pint sized pony was allowed in the paddock. Although several of the other trainers complained about the pint sized horse, as long as she remained quiet and out of everyone's way, she could stay.

*****

As the starting gate opened there was a cavalry charge to the front as four fillies fought for the early lead. A Kadabra filly named *Kadie Kadabra* reached the quarter pole in a speedy 26 seconds.

Before the half there was a change of leader three times—thus they reached the half in a very fast 54 seconds. Elena had been sitting sixth the whole mile when Jack tipped her past the ¾ pole.

At the top of the stretch the filly went three wide as she breezed by the horses ahead of her, setting a new track record for three-year-old trotting fillies in 1:52.1.

The next four legs of the Gold, Elena had three wins and one second—that one she lost by a nose.

"*I can't believe how good our girl is this year,*" Jackie told Mr. C. at the barn after the race.

"*I was worried if she would hold up, but she is better now than she has ever been.*"

"*That's good, Jack, because I am going to supplement her to the Maple Leaf Trot,*" Mr. C. said.

Jack dropped his helmet when he heard what Charamblos said.

"*WHAT! Are you kidding me? That race is for the colts and aged horses.*" "*Please don't do that to Elena,*" Jack begged.

"*I'm sorry Jack, but I have given this a lot of thought. I have a strong feeling about this. I don't expect to win, but maybe she will get a third or a fourth, and that's a hell of a lot of money.*"

"*I have faith in her. She's my baby girl,*" Mr. C. said as he kissed Elena on her nose. "*I'm not going to change my mind.*"

*****

"What did I just hear? I have to race against the boys?"

"Please let me race, Jack. Maybe I will get to see my brother, Junior."

"And you should have more faith in me or else I will demand a change of drivers," Elena mumbled as she munched her hay.

"Don't worry, Elena. I will be right by your side and no matter what you do in the big race, you will always be a winner to me!" Bessy said.

*****

On Saturday, July 6, it had been raining on and off all day, making for a very sloppy track for the three-year-old trotting colts.

"I can't believe how bad the weather is. I would scratch Junior but he can go as fast on a sloppy track as he can on a fast one. He already proved that," Chris told Stefan.

Just then Emma walked in the barn. *"Hey, dad, did you hear the news? Junior's sister Elena won the final last night in the Gold and set a new track record."*

Although Emma lived with her mom Joanne and Jack, she remained close to her father and visited him often at his barn.

"Boy she is something this year, isn't she? I'm so glad she came back good for Jack."

"And guess what? Dad called me last night and told me he is supplementing the filly to the Maple Leaf Trot," Chris said.

"You've got to be kidding! I mean I know she is a really good filly— but racing against the boys---that's another thing," Stefan answered.

"I know there's been a few mares who have shown the boys a thing or two in the past like Bee A Magician and Hannelore Hanover, but they are few and far between," Chris stated.

"Do you really think she can beat her brother Junior, let alone all the other tough colts? Hell, I wouldn't even race Junior in that race if Mr. C. didn't have his heart set on it."

"Did you get a look at the colts that are eligible? That monster four-year-old, Puccio is undefeated this year."

"I know your grandpa wants to race Junior in the race, but if it were

up to me, I wouldn't. That's' really, really hard, racing a three-year-old against older more experienced colts."

"I think he keeps forgetting that both Elena and Junior have modest breeding. They are going to have to race against the likes of Muscle Hills and Kadabras."

"I know these two are super good, but come on now, they aren't SUPER STARS!" Chris laughed.

*****

"Hey, wait a minute here. Don't I have something to say about this? After all I was the "Two-Year-Old Trotting Colt of the Year." And I have beaten the odds ever since I was born. So give me some credit here, won't you!" Junior thought.

"I told you I'm the Rocky Balboa of harness racing. I am no longer an underdog!"

"Now, let the games begin!" Junior scoffed.

"Well, before I let dad enter Junior in the Maple Leaf, he best win every Gold race or at least be right there," Chris laughed.

"Well if that's all I have to do, so be it. If it means I get to see my sister, Elena again, my God I will do my best, just wait and see," thought Junior.

And that's just what "the brother from another mother" did. He easily swept the Gold for trotting colts and did it in impressively.

12

We Meet Again

"You were my once in a lifetime connection. We were destined to meet, no matter the distance between us and we will return to each other again and again."

Fall 2019
Mohawk Racetrack
Ontario, Canada

After the final of the Gold Series, *Fleetwood* was voted "Three-Year-Old Trotter of the Year." With a record of 8-2-0 in 12 starts during his brief two year career and amassing $800,000 there was no doubt in Mr. C.'s mind that the orphan colt could be a serious contender in the upcoming Maple Leaf Trot which would take place in October.

"I can't believe our boy will be racing in the most prestigious race in Canada. We will be going for $700,000 dollars!" Chris told Stefan.

"I know. It boggles my mind to even think about that. From this minute on I will not leave my boy—not even for one second. There will be a lot of jealous people and since our boy is one of the one's to beat, you can't trust anybody."

"In fact, I'm going to sleep in front of his stall every night. I already bought a cot," the Swede replied.

"Don't you think you're going a little too far, Stefan? I mean I know *we have to watch him, but sleeping here every night?"* laughed Chris. *"It gets downright cold in the barn at night."*

"No, I don't think I'm being over cautious. In fact, I have someone I want you to meet," Stefan said as he went out to his car.

When Stefan returned he had a black German Shepherd dog with him.

"I want you to meet Sam, Fleetwoods' own personal body guard. He will take over watching him when I have to go to the men's room, shower, or grab a bite to eat."

Chris jumped back for just the sight of the ferocious dog was enough to keep anyone away.

"Hey, I think you're going a little too far here, Stefan. I mean I have to work in the barn, and so do the other grooms."

"Don't worry. He is as gentle as a lamb with his own. But God help anyone who doesn't belong in here," Stefan scowled.

Luckily for everyone, Stefan was right. Sam was a pleasure to be around for Team Christoforou and loved Junior, and vice versa.

When the groom and colt would go out for their daily walks or Junior would be turned out in his paddock, Sam would be right there with him.

And if anyone dared to come near the paddock the Shepherd would scare them away quickly, curling his lip and showing his sharp teeth.

For the next several weeks, things were quite nerve wracking at the Christoforou Stable as they prepared for their very first Maple Leaf Trot.

The media was quick to judge and had written several disparaging articles that displeased Jack, Chris and Mr. C.

Jackie Mo may have been a taskmaster with his stable crew, his second trainers, business associates and what have you, but with his personal staff he was proper and generous. And when it came to anyone talking bad about any of his "four-legged-kids" he was a tyrant!

The media dubbed *Fleetwood "an underdog who got lucky,"* and *Peristera "a good-looking filly who will get her lunch in the Maple Leaf."*

The week before the Maple Leaf was run, a journalist in the local newspaper wrote an article about the upcoming race and the eleven competitors.

He praised the four-year-old favorite, Puccio, who would be coming from position nine.

"The nine hole won't hurt this colt, for not only is he undefeated, but this is the softest field I have seen in years," wrote the editor.

"It's a lock for Puccio as he takes on the likes of an orphan, who although has been racing well and got lucky accumulating almost $800,000, Fleetwood, will get himself a new a-hole in the Maple Leaf."

"And the lone filly, Peristera, who shared her dams teets with Fleetwood as foals.... Where is Charamblos Christoforou's head? It takes a lot to make a good horse and some of the most important requisites do not appear on the surface."

"Yeah, Peristera is a fine looking filly, but many a good-looking horse is a counterfeit. And racing against the mares is a lot different than racing against the colts," he wrote.

When Mr. C. read the paper he told Jack and his son, Chris, *"We gotta show this S.O.B. that we are as good as this Puccio, Guccio---whatever the hell his name is."*

"Whatever you do, have my two kids ready to show them what they're mad of."

*****

The pressure was on so Chris decided to change his training strategy. He trained Junior at Mohawk the week of the big race and went a mile and a half--something he never did with the colt before.

Three days before the big race, Chris, Junior, and Sam shipped to Mohawk to train the colt, prepping for the big race.

He trained Junior a mile and a half in 2:20—last half in 58.4. The colt looked better than he ever had.

As Stefan was stripping him for his bath, Jamie from the Jack Moiseyev Stable was walking in *Persitera*-- the only filly entered in the prestigious race.

Stefan had heard the incredible story of Junior as a foal and that it was in fact *Peristera's* dam who took the orphan colt in as her own. He also knew that Junior and Elena were two peas in a pod and had been closer than close.

When Jamie walked Elena past Junior, the filly stopped and would go no further. The mare just stood there looking over at Junior creating strange noises.

Startled, Junior pushed through the cross ties and cocked his ears with a surprised look on his face. He responded to Elena with incomprehensible sounds that Stefan never heard the colt make before.

Doing his job of protecting the colt, Sam, the Shepherd began growling at Jamie and Elena. Immediately Chris calmed the dog and securely tied him in the corner. Meanwhile, Bessy who was walking by Elena, became very irritated and started bucking and kicking.

"Jamie you better take Bessy and tie her in the stall across the way. We certainly don't need any problems now," Joanne said.

Once the pony was taken away and Sam settled down, the two horses seemed to be continuing their conversation. As they were producing sounds that only they could understand, Stefan, Chris, Jack, Jamie and Joanne stood there in disbelief.

"Junior, is that you? I have thought about you for so long and have been worried about you. My have you grown! You always were a handsome boy, but now you are a gorgeous man!" Elena snorted.

"Yes, Elena. It's me— your baby brother. And you—look at you! You are breathtaking. You are the most beautiful thing I have ever laid eyes on. And I also have thought about you, over and over again," replied Junior.

"What are you doing here? I heard them talking and they said you are the best three-year-old trotting colt in the country. I'm sooooo proud of you. Mama would be, too. Both of your mamas I mean," laughed Elena.

"Thanks. I did it all for you and mama. Both of them!"

"Every race I told myself I had to win to make you guys proud, and I did." the colt said.

"And I heard Joanne talking saying that you got hurt last year. I was so worried that you wouldn't be okay."

"Then Jack told Chris that you came back super this year and you are almost undefeated! Thank God you are well. I am so proud of you, too."

"No worries little brother. Yeah I did hurt my leg, but Jamie worked on it and now I'm like new."

"I have a little companion named Bessy that takes good care of me. You met her in the paddock that day. She's not you, but she's the next best thing," Elena laughed.

*****

"Okay you two, that's enough now. We are here to work. Now come on Elena let's get out there and train," Jackie Mo said.

As Jamie led Elena out on the track, the two horses locked eyes and seemed to say goodbye in their own special way.

That day Elena trained the best she had ever trained in her life, going a mile in 1:55.

"Wow! This little girl is ready to show the boys what she's made of," Jack told Joanne as he got off the bike.

"Yea, I never saw her look so good. Perhaps we should have her visit her brother before the race next week," laughed Joanne.

"Hey, I never thought about that. But they are both going to be racing against one another. How about that!"

"I sure hope that's a good thing," Jack said.

That night after the horses were settled in their stalls, Stefan and Sam fell fast asleep outside of Junior's stall. After all was quiet, Junior stood in the back of his stall reminiscing.

"Elena. It was so good seeing you today. I love you as much as I ever have. I hope we see one another again soon," Junior thought.

Several barns over, as Bessy the pony found her spot in the stall to retire, Elena thought, *"My baby brother. I am so happy that we saw each other. You have grown into a handsome strong colt. Your mama would have been so proud. And our mama would be, too. Remember I will always love you."*

13

Dreams Do Come True

"Dreams Do Come True-- If We Only Wish Hard Enough"

October 2019
Campbelville, Ontario
Mohawk Racetrack

The intermittently fickle Mother Nature had been surprisingly cooperative in Campbellville, Ontario. Saturday, September 7, was a pleasant 75 degrees with but a hint of breeze, and for all intents a picture perfect day for horseracing.

It was the day thousands of horsemen, racing fans, owners and trainers had been anxiously waiting all year for. It was Maple Leaf Day.

Significantly, Maple Leaf Day is when Ontario's finest trotters, both male and female, are on display taking on the best the North American continent has to offer by competing in such prestigious events as *The Peaceful Way, The Wellwood Memorial, The Elegant Image, The Canadian Trotting Classic,* and of course *The Maple Leaf Trot,* a race that is open to all comers.

Maple Leaf Day in Canada is comparable to the Kentucky Derby that is held annually in Louisville, Kentucky for the best equine athletes compete for millions of dollars in purse money, along with the prestigious title.

Race secretary Scott McKelvie did a superb job putting

together an outstanding racing card featuring the best trotters the sport has to offer. Headlining todays thirteen-race program is The Canadian Trotting Classic for three-year-olds, and the Maple Leaf Trot for older trotters.

Along with the Trotting Classic and The Maple Leaf Trot is the Elegant Image—a race where sophomore trotting fillies will compete for almost $500,000---- while freshman trotting fillies will race in the $350,000 William Wellwood Memorial.

Today's race is not much different than the initial inaugural Maple Leaf Trot held in 1950, other than the field of eleven today has some of the finest trotters Mohawk Racetrack has ever seen. And the purse money has escalated from the $5,000 Morris Mite was awarded in 1950 to almost $700,000---of which $350,000 the lucky victor will take home today.

*****

At daybreak, tepid dawning haze peered over the roof of the Mohawk Racetrack grandstand while a ray of sunshine lingered on the infield. Throughout the week leading up to the big day, grooms were seen carrying sloshing buckets to waiting horses in rustling straw-strewn stalls in what is known as 'the detention barn', but politely termed 'the stake's barn.'

Traditionally, equine contenders in major events are isolated in the stakes barn as mandated by the racing commission, as they are ever vigilant to ensure that no horse receives an unfair medicinal advantage.

All week long those that inhabited the Mohawk racing office, plus a handful of Press Box regulars had been buzzing over the possibility that *Peristera* and *Fleetwood*, (formerly known as Elena and Junior) respectively the best three-year-old Ontario sired filly and colt, would disdain entering their respective divisional classics-- The Elegant Image and Canadian Trotting Classic. Instead, both the colt and filly shared by the same owner, Charalamblos Christoforou, but trained in different stables, would be entered in The Maple Leaf.

At first glance that seemed an ambitious undertaking to say

the least, but then *Peristera* and *Fleetwood* have overcome virtually insurmountable odds since inception.

Unlike events exclusive to certain age groups, The Maple Leaf Trot has long been carded as a race for three-year-olds and older. Thus, occasionally the younger set had been asked to compete against their elders; though it would seem the "youth" had best be of considerable prowess to attempt such an undertaking.

It was remembered that *In Free*, better known as the dam of *Governor Armbro*, won the Maple Leaf as a three-year-old in 1957, and *Supergrit* did it in 1997-- also at three.

Could *Peristera* and *Fleetwood* be in a league with *In Free* and *Supergrit*? That remains to be seen. But both horses have been ultra impressive versus their age group peers thus far this year as they each have an almost perfect record on the Ontario Gold Circuit.

When interviewed by Dave Briggs for the Globe and Mail, owner Charalamblos Christoforou/aka Mr. C. conceded that stepping up from the Ontario Gold Circuit to the Maple Leaf level is indeed a serious escalation.

"But then I've never owned a colt or a filly like either one of these two before."

He continued, *"Ever since they were foaled it's been one miracle after another, and although one or both may be overmatched, I felt compelled to give them the opportunity. Of course, they'll be racing against each other for the first time and unfortunately only one of them can win—but that'll be up to them, and out of my hands."*

*****

The Maple Leaf Trot was first launched in 1950 at Thorncliffe Park Raceway in Leaside, Ontario, when *Adeline Hanover* and *Morris Mite* finished in a dead-heat after each horse respectively won their division. Since there would be no third heat race-off, a coin toss was done, awarding *Morris Mite* the trophy.

In 1954, The Maple Leaf Trot moved to Old Woodbine and stayed there until 1994 when the race re-located to Woodbine Racetrack where it remained until 2001. For the past 18 years the running of the Maple Leaf Classic has been held as part of Mohawk Raceway's summer stakes extravaganza.

The Maple Leaf Trot is not age restricted and is predominately known for its male champions, but there have been some mares that have won throughout the years--- including the great *Delmonica Hanover* in 1975.

Twelve years later in 1987 it was *Franconia*, then it would be a long 28 years before the unparalleled *Bee A Magician* would "kick the boys to the curb" in 2015.

In that the Maple Leaf is held every year, there have been multiple winners, namely *Tie Silk, No Sex Please, Grandpa Jim* and *San Pail* that have each won the coveted trophy three times. This is a huge feat for just winning it once is commendable, considering the race annually attracts the premier trotters in active racing.

In today's race three-year-old filly *Peristera* will try her luck in adding to the list of these champion mares, but first she will have to beat out ten rather chauvinistic male colts and geldings.

Peristera who will start from post two will be drove by her trainer Jack Moiseyev (Jackie Mo), and if victorious it will be Jackie Mo's second win in the Maple Leaf Trot, having won with *Fools Goal* in 2002.

Chris Christoforou, Jr., trainer/driver for the three-year-old colt *Fleetwood*, has yet to actually bring home a Maple Leaf trophy.

Chris will pilot his 9 to 2 morning line third choice, *Fleetwood*. The colt will leave from post seven.

The remaining field includes: from the rail out, *Musclemania, Peristera, Another Day, Justin Jones, Mr. Muscles, Kadabradabra, Fleetwood, Alwaysagent, Puccio* and *Gravity* is on the extreme outside from post ten. Rounding out the field is *Tomorrowsalock* from post 11, leaving from the second tier.

The morning line favorite is the undefeated four-year-old gelding, Puccio, who set the record for trotting geldings last month in the Cashman Memorial at the Meadowlands. His seasonal earnings approach $1 million.

Second choice is the Muscle Hill four-year-old, Mr. Muscles who has an impressive 8 wins out of 12 starts this year.

Three-year-old *Fleetwood*, the third choice, has come on strongly lately, lowering the famous *Trixton*'s 1:50.2 Hambletonian record at The Meadowlands. He has amassed $800,000 plus on his card.

And then there's the lone filly, *Peristera*. It was touch and go all year whether *Peristera* by E.L.Titan would even be nominated, as she had been lightly raced at two, having competed in only one baby race which she won handily in 1:56.1. Thereafter, she was stopped after sustaining a minor but nagging injury.

As a three-year-old *Peristera* came back in 2019 with a vengeance and now sports an impressive 3 wins in 5 starts, including a brilliant 1:50.3 tally at Mohawk last month. Thus, owner Christoforou had no second thoughts of supplementing his pride and joy filly for the Maple Leaf Trot.

*****

At 5:30 p.m. sharp the doors opened to the grandstand quickly filling with the usual regulars and more than a smattering of celebrities that were on hand to partake in the big race spectacle and festivities. After all, Maple Leaf night comes but once a year.

Governor David Johnson, pop singer Justin Bieber, comedian Jim Carrey and actor Ryan Gosling---all homebred Canadians and their entourages were there to watch the big race.

You could feel the pulsating excitement that feverishly flowed through the air and the tension among the owners and trainers was so thick you needed the proverbial chef's knife to slice through.

When the national anthem "O Canada" sounded across the loudspeaker, many in the grandstand rose and sang along.

But during the post parade something unexpected happened. While the eleven equine athletes were parading in post-position order, *Peristera* began acting up. Her caretaker, Jamie, rushed to the track to calm the anxious filly, as driver Jackie Mo immediately hopped out of the sulky to assist.

"What's going on with Elena? She never acts like this!" questioned a worried Jackie Mo. *"Is her equipment on right? Is the bit bothering her?"*

As #7, *Fleetwood*, trotted up to *Peristera*, the brown colt planted his hooves and refused to go another step.

"What the hell?" bellowed Chris.

The two horses stood there almost frozen side-by-side as the filly and colt started nickering. With interlocking eyes *Peristera* produced a blood-curdling whinny as she seemed to be conversing directly to *Fleetwood*. The colt answered back, but in a far more calming tone.

"Oh my God. They remember each other. I can't believe it!" stammered Jack.

*****

As the two horses stood there forcing a slight delay, some onlookers stared in disbelief. After a few final snorts and whimpers, both competitors sufficiently calmed permitting their drivers to rejoin the others, now scoring down in their final warm ups in the backstretch.

The starter called the field and the gate opened as the 2019 Maple Leaf prepared for a start.

Would it be Puccio, the undefeated gelding? Peristera, the only filly, or the orphan colt, Fleetwood, who would take home the trophy and the title of 2019 Winner of the Maple Leaf Trot?

*****

The grandstand was packed and there wasn't an empty seat in the dining room. Sitting up front by the glass window across from the finish line was Mr. C., the Storfers, Emma, and several friends.

Both the celebrated orphan colt and his sister had their share of local supporters. Many who had visited them at nearby High Stakes Farm were there to cheer on their favorite horse.

*****

It was now post time.

When Elena trotted in front of the grandstand, the crowd

went wild—some holding banners reading "Girl Power" and "Show the boys, Elena."

Seconds later Junior paraded proudly trotting by as if he was saying, "Hey, look me over."

Fans held signs that read, "The orphan is King," and "Anything is possible."

As the horses lined up behind the gate for the 2019 Maple Leaf Trot, the crowd tensed. Around the first turn, the favorite, Puccio made a nasty break and trailed the field by daylight as disgruntled bettors roared with disgust.

After Chris noticed the favorite breaking, he let Fleetwood ease out under his own power, easily grabbing the lead.

Peristera got away fifth as she was sandwiched in by several outside leavers.

Fleetwood got to the quarter in a very fast 25.4 seconds, much more than Chris wanted to go, but the driver was just along for the ride as Fleetwood was doing it strictly on his own.

Before the half, Musclemania pulled off the rail, challenging Fleetwood as they reached the half in a very fast 53 seconds.

When Fleetwood looked Musclemania in the eye, he toyed with him a bit, letting his rival think he was done.

Fleetwood then put in that extra gear he always saved for late in the mile, reaching the three-quarter's in 1:21.2.

"*They're on world record tempo,*" the announcer screamed.

As Chris and Fleetwood pulled away from Musclemania, Peristera shook free from the five hole, passing several horses on the far outside.

"*And down the stretch they come!*" "*It's pandemonium –pure bedlam.*"

As his two homebreds fought down the lane, Mr. C. stood up shouting, "*Come on Junior. Come on Elena!*"

Emma was hysterical, not knowing who to cheer for. Jamie and Stefan glued to the monitor in the paddock were ecstatic, each urging their own horse on.

"*It's Fleetwood on the inside. Persitera is gaining on the outside.*"

"*Forget the rest. It's a two horse race—Fleetwood and Peristera.*"

113

"Peristera and Fleetwood."

"Peristera is gaining, but Fleetwood is holding safe."

Approaching the wire Fleetwood and Peristera turned their heads and saw each other.

"Elena. Oh my God, is that you?" Junior yelled.

"Yes, it's me. Oh no. I don't want to beat you, Junior."

"And I can't beat you, Elena."

Both Jackie and Chris knew something very strange was happening for their steeds were once again making those strange noises and looking at one another, but never missed a beat trotting.

As they crossed the finish line Ken Middleton bellowed, *"Ladies and gentlemen, it is too close to call. Today you have witnessed a world record of 1:48.2 in the Maple Leaf."*

"It's a photo finish between Peristera and Fleetwood, otherwise known as Elena and Junior –the brother and sister who shared one of the most incredible love stories ever."

"Hold ALL tickets."

"This may take awhile as they were whiskers apart."

14

The Celebration of Two Champions

"True Love Stories Never Have Endings."

October, 2019
Ontario, Canada

Almost synchronized, Peristera and Fleetwood crossed the finish line together. It was way too close to call, so a photo finish picture was sent to be developed. Some of the fans called Peristera as the victor, while others swore Fleetwood got it.

The agonizing ten minutes required to get the print posted seemed like hours for all involved. Could this be a repeat of when Adeline Hanover and Morris Mite finished in a dead heat in the Maple Leaf Trot at Thorncliffe Park in 1950? If so, one thing for sure is there would be no coin toss this time to decide the winner.

"I think you got it," Jackie Mo said to Chris as they were waiting for the results.

"No, I think you caught me at the wire by a hair," laughed Chris.

"Boy, did your mare race super. I thought we were home free, then that little girl appeared out of nowhere!"

Both the colt and filly raced incredibly, shattering the previous record of 1:49 set by the great *Sebastian K.*

As everyone waited nervously waited for the photo, Stefan was pacing back and forth while Jamie prayed, each waiting to grab their respective horses.

It seemed that the only ones not nervous were the two horses.

"I hope you won, Junior. You raced a hell of a race, brother," Elena said.

"No, I hope you won, Elena. YOU are the one who raced a monster mile coming from the back. When I saw it was you I eased up a bit because I didn't want to beat you."

"It reminded me of when we were weanlings running in the field, racing to see who could run the fastest. And Elena you always won," laughed Junior.

"That's because you let me win, didn't you?" Elena laughed.

The crowd got quiet as announcer Middleton breathlessly articulated over the loud speaker, *"Ladies and gentlemen. Tonight you have witnessed history. The sister and brother by another mother finished in a dead heat setting a new world record!"*

The crowd erupted, *"Elena and Junior! Junior and Elena!"*

As the two horses returned to the winners circle, waiting there for the new champions to return were Emma, Mr. C., the Storfers, Stefan, Jamie, friends and family. Director of racing, Mark McKelvie was also there proudly holding two trophies— one for each horse.

Joanne steered her parade pony to the winner circle and dismounted, throwing her arms around him and giving Jack a big kiss.

When Peristera and Fleetwood returned, Jamie and Stefan turned them so they faced each other. Slowly, Elena walked up to Junior and placed her nose right on his, the exact moment the photographer snapped the winning photo.

To Be Continued...

Epilogue

Sadly, we live in a disturbing world today–one that is filled with violence, hatred and sadness. Whenever we come across a story like the one about Elena and Junior, it brings joy to our hearts and hope for the future.

Fairy tales have been with us for centuries. The timeless stories of Cinderella, Sleeping Beauty, Little Red Riding Hood, Rapunzel, Black Beauty and Beauty and the Beast are truly universal and have been around for years and will still be with us for years to come.

Fairy tale characters inspire us to cheer for them because in our minds they're human and alive and when we look at them we see ourselves.

Perhaps we enjoy fairytales because they make us joyful and have happy endings and maybe happy endings are exactly what people need to believe. People need to have creativity, imagination, and love, in order to become the artists, inventors, and humanitarians of tomorrow.

People need hope—they need to have a tomorrow. And although fairy tales certainly aren't solely responsible for this, they certainly are an inspiration.

Fairy tales remind us to dream, because everyone deserves their own *"Happily ever after."*

The story of Junior and Elena is a fairy tale come true. It is about hope, determination, willpower and most of all LOVE--- the unconditional love we all hope to experience at least once in our lifetimes.

Although their story is factual, we don't know exactly how

their career in racing will materialize, but as I said I am a dreamer and a hopeless romantic. Whether or not these two incredible animals develop into racehorses and how good they will be is something we will have to wait and see.

But for now Junior and Elena are growing into beautiful adult horses that will forever share a bond and an incredible beautiful story.

A story that inspires us to believe in the impossible and that *Dreams Do Come True!*

About The Author

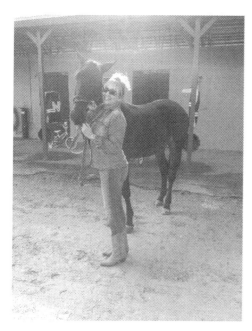

Victoria M. Howard is an internationally published author. Her first book, *Why Women Love Bad Boys* has been translated and sold in 15 countries.

She holds several beauty titles and once represented her state in the Mrs. USA Pageant. In 2011 she was awarded "VIP Woman of the Year" by Who's Who Women Worldwide.

Ms. Howard has trained, bred and raced standardbreds for forty years and currently lives in Florida where she visits her four-legged babies.

Acknowledgements

I would like to thank Joanne Colville, Emma Christoforou, Charamblos Christoforou, Jackie Moiseyev, and Chris Christoforou for giving me permission to write this remarkable story.

Special thanks to Gerry De Bresser-Colville, Joanne Colville, and Shirley McLean for the use of the horse photos.

And a very special thanks to Bob Marks.

Printed in the United States
By Bookmasters